A Sociological Yearbook of Religion in Britain · 3

A Sociological Yearbook of Religion in Britain · 3

Edited by David Martin
& Michael Hill

SCM PRESS LTD

This book has been produced in co-operation with
Socio-Religious Research Services

ι^c

0334 01570 7

*First published 1970
by SCM Press Ltd
56 Bloomsbury Street London WC1*

© *SCM Press Ltd 1970*

*Printed in Great Britain by
Billing & Sons Limited
Guildford and London*

CONTENTS

THE CONTRIBUTORS

NICHOLAS ABERCROMBIE, JOHN BAKER, SEBASTIAN BRETT, JANE FOSTER   Sometime post-graduate students at the London School of Economics and Political Science

DAVID B. CLARK   Methodist Minister. Secretary, Methodist Sociological Group, 22a Dartmouth Road, London S.E.10

ROBERT W. COLES   Institute of Social and Economic Research, University of York

CLIFFORD HILL   Congregational Minister. Senior Lecturer in Sociology, Barking Regional College of Technology

MICHAEL HILL   Lecturer in Sociology, London School of Economics and Political Science

ROGER HOMAN   University of Sussex

BERNICE MARTIN   Lecturer in Sociology, Bedford College, University of London

DAVID MARTIN   Reader in Sociology, London School of Economics and Political Science

MARGARET SCOTFORD ARCHER   Lecturer in Sociology, University of Reading

PETER D. VARNEY   Anglican Priest. Research Secretary, Church of England Missionary and Ecumenical Council

MICHALINA VAUGHAN   Lecturer in Sociology, London School of Economics and Political Science

ROBIN H. WARD   Lecturer in Sociology, University of Manchester

PREFACE

IN THIS issue we pursue the same policy as in the previous two issues of including papers on a variety of topics likely to interest different but overlapping constituencies. We have also included broader theoretical articles when these might reasonably have relevance to modern Britain: in the first issue such an article concerned 'cults' and in the second issue Christian–Marxist relations. In the present issue the theoretical article concerns secularization theory with special reference to the key institutional area of education. The article on the Rome Symposium also deals with broader issues. The large piece on superstition is in part a response to an editorial plea a couple of years ago for some information about this area of belief in contemporary Britain. We are convinced that the bibliography prepared by Robert Coles will prove useful, and it is intended to keep this continually updated.

Indeed, it has already raised a somewhat wider problem. There seems to be some truth in the definition of sociology as 'the study of people who don't need studying by people who do', at least among some sociologists of religion. Towards the end of last year several interested participants quite spontaneously felt a sense of *anomie*, which has previously been reserved for those under the microscope. In particular, it was felt that since the sociology of British religion is such a fast-growing area, there was increasingly a need for some kind of organized bibliography and reporting of current research. Robert Coles and Colin Campbell at York and Michael Hill at LSE have been working on the problem, and a conference was held in York at the beginning of November. It is hoped that the Yearbook can play an important role, especially since it aims to tap a rather wider field than do most of the specialized sociological journals.

Already the policy of the Yearbook has been established as a form of enlightened eclecticism, and this will continue in the next issue which should include articles on such divergent topics as utopian communities, church organizations in Liverpool and Scotland, and the role of women in the different Christian churches. As from the next issue Michael Hill will be sole editor and will be most interested

Preface

to receive any articles and suggestions relating to the general area
covered by the Yearbook.

DAVID MARTIN
MICHAEL HILL
*The London School of Economics
and Political Science*

1 Rome and the Sociologists

David Martin

THE calling of a conference in Rome on 'The Culture of Unbelief' was important for sociology and as some indication of the seriousness with which the church is prepared to consider the contributions of the social sciences, however tentative these may be. The Secretariat for Non-Believers is one of the smaller Vatican secretariats set up after the Council, and this occasion was its first major public effort. It occurred with the co-operation of the Department of Sociology at Berkeley, California and with the financial assistance of the Agnelli Foundation of Turin. The Agnelli Foundation was formed in 1966 as an Italian equivalent of the Ford and Nuffield Foundations to sponsor a wide range of activities and is itself an interesting development. Since the Italian universities are in frequent chaos there is some feeling that scholarship may sometimes have to find a base outside them.

At any rate for sociology, for the Secretariat and for the Foundation the opening of the conference was itself quite an event. Apart from an apparatus of television and cameras worthy of satire by Fellini, the first meeting was a 'round table' discussion in the main hall of the Gregorian University attended by six cardinals and some 3,000 people. Cardinal Koenig presided over an exchange of views between Harvey Cox, Jean Danielou, and Professor Manchevic of the Charles University, Prague. The course of the conference was punctuated by frequent television appearances by those involved; and a papal seal was set to the occasion by the members of the symposium meeting with the Pope when he took the opportunity personally to support any effort by the church to understand its position in contemporary society. Another kind of papal blessing was provided by the participation of the doyen of contemporary sociology, Professor Talcott Parsons of Harvard.

The main purpose of this article is to indicate the main themes of the symposium; but something should be said about the composition and organization of the conference. The chairman was Peter Berger, with three discussion groups chaired by Sabino Aquaviva (Padua), Thomas O'Dea (California), and David Martin (LSE). Three papers were prepared by Thomas Luckmann (Frankfort), Robert Bellah (California), and Charles Glock (California). Replies to these papers were prepared by Oleg Mandic (a Marxist philosopher from Zagreb) Martin Marty (Chicago), and Bryan Wilson (Oxford). Broadly they were designed to move from conceptual problems on to developmental concerns and finally to concrete research, whether of the survey type or institutional analysis. The participants were principally sociologists, with an occasional social psychologist (Professor Vergote of Louvain), and a sprinkling of theologians, notably René Marlé and Henri de Lubac.

Something of the broad aims of the conference may be suggested by a division proposed by one of the participants, Benton Johnson, into those with a European bias and the Americans. This was best illustrated in the vigorous contrast between Bellah as an American Quaker and Isambert as a French Catholic. Crudely there were those – the Europeans – who for the purposes of the conference defined religion in terms of institutional complexes and certain varieties of more or less coherent 'belief' generally of a transcendental kind,[1] and those – the Americans – who saw it as a 'system of relevance' (Luckmann) or a free symbolization of authentic personal being (Bellah). There was a tendency for those with these alternative definitional preferences either to accept or to reject the likelihood of coherent institutional and coherent belief systems maintaining themselves into the future. The 'Americans' (with flourishing religious institutions but pluralistic and individualistic ideology) tended to anticipate increased privatization, and saw institutional religion and coherent beliefs as an earlier stage of development. As a matter of fact, this characterization is a considerable simplification: Thomas Luckmann and Thomas O'Dea, for example, played quite opposite roles; but then, O'Dea is a practising Catholic as well as an American.

This is perhaps the point to introduce two controversies which were only partly definitional: firstly that arising from Bellah's paper and secondly that arising from Luckmann's paper. The first turned partly on Bellah's definition, but also on the way this definition was linked to his evolutionary scheme and vision of the future. The second turned partly on Luckmann's definition, partly on the complex question of functional equivalence to which it gave rise, and partly on his evolutionary scheme.

Perhaps I should say in parenthesis that what follows is less an objective report than an angled shot of matters which particularly interested me.

With regard to Bellah's important and interesting paper, there were certain organizing themes to be discerned in his basic approach: the limited historical area in space and time of belief conceived as cognition, the growth of the free intelligentsia, the growth of freedom from external authorities, and the increase in freedom of religious choice. It was the first free intelligentsia of Greece which initially conceived of belief in cognitive terms and therefore first 'disbelieved': it is the modern intelligentsia which releases religion from cognitive chains and sees it as 'truth' embodied in image, enactment and narrative, this being in any case the predominant style of biblical religion as well as of Far Eastern religion. When faith was linked to orthodoxy and dogma (i.e. to belief) this was because religion was rooted in social hierarchy and the maintenance of authority. When no longer joined to cognition, to orthodoxy and to authority it ceases to conflict with science and no longer needs to 'double' for the political authority. Further than this, the quest for inwardness involves on the one hand the possibility of 'privatization' but, on the other hand, plays into the possibility of 'genuine sympathetic groups' and of 'vast value consensus' at odds not only with loyalty to the nation, but with any particular loyalty or boundary such as that of a church. Secularization can only take place with respect to religion as social control,[2] as specific coherent institutions linked to specific beliefs; it cannot take place with respect to religion as awareness of common humanity, as commitment and vision and as awareness of the antinomies of man's being. So far as these latter are concerned the twentieth century may be the most religious ever; they are indeed being 'generalized as the dominant conception of religion in modern society'. America illustrates and anticipates this unbounded new religion of integrity and the free spirit in its anti-war movement and in the Peace Corps. 'All believe something', and 'vision' is distributed within and without organized churches.

This view was attacked: as methodologically unsound since it made the area of study simply co-extensive with the variations in personal authenticity, as highly speculative in so far as it embodied an evolutionary scheme, and as celebrating some presumed value consensus in 'religion' roughly equivalent to the end of ideology in politics as discerned by American political scientists.[3] Indeed, the whole notion looked highly American in its dual stress on highly developed individuation and in the conception of an incipient Religion of Humanity (Comtean too, of course); and equally it appeared American in its assumption that America (and further, certain groups in America) could stand in as the harbinger of evolutionary development to come. For Professor O'Dea this was intellectual Coca-Colonization; for David Martin, Bellah was providing these groups with the same kind of pathfinder status as the élite segment of the working class possessed in Marxism. Like Luckmann, Bellah largely ignored contemporary communism, i.e. the massive fact of vast areas where a political orthodoxy is promulgated which forcibly *privatizes* traditional religion and which assumes it is right and others wrong both in a philosophical and in a cognitive sense. The majority of mankind is presumably as much in favour of humanity as it is against 'sin': it just happens to have fundamentally different notions about the beliefs and institutions which will embody this ideal. If the definition of religion is simply restricted to this vague ideal and the radically alternative modes of implementation ignored then sure enough nearly everybody is religious and most people are agreed.

This critique was developed by Martin Marty, David Martin, F. A. Isambert and Thomas O'Dea, who *inter alia* suggested that truth-claims did matter, that radically different orientations not only existed currently, but would continue to exist in the nature of society, and that this was not due to a failure to 'understand' or to being – as Professor Bellah suggested – in some way personally retarded ('hung-up') at an earlier stage of development. Instead, it was suggested that successive stages such as those described by Bellah did not necessarily replace each other, even after an interim period of confusion and co-existence, but rather that they extended the range of options *without* replacing the forms previously important. Indeed, far from being a passing and regrettable phase one could view the distinctive institutionalization, the objective reference, the dogmatic coherence, the radical posing of alternatives found in Christianity as part of the 'cutting edge' of modernity: some forms might be obsolete but the syncretistic and subjectivist alternative hardly represented an advance. For Professor Isambert the sharp edge of Christian faith introduced a 'contestation' and therefore 'unbelief'.

Marxism was one form taken by this unbelief and one should not wriggle out of 'contestation' by defining unbelief out of existence and then sprinkling holy water on it.

Professor O'Dea developed the critique further. He argued that the 'id' was central to most subjectivist religion and that it provided no criteria for the desirable and undesirable, and could easily develop into instinctualism. The rhetoric which contrasted known truth with embodied truth was too facile. So too was the contrast between repressive authority and genuine faith. Reality was more paradoxical and complex. The history of the Roman Church was not simply one of successful repression, but one in which authority protected and defended faith as well as faith being used as a protective device for authority. The sacramental system combined objectivity *and* deep internalised faith, for example the sacrament of penance. Professor Bellah had not only imposed American notions of cultural convergence on the movement of history but had imposed his own eschatology on history as well.

There were further points, both analytic and historical. David Martin, for example, was critical of Bellah's notion that one could no more define Christianity than define religion. Bellah's view reduced Christianity to an amorphous dynamic which had no central tendencies or continuing core: in that case there was no possibility of separating believer from unbeliever within *any* period, and *every* change from one period to another became a crisis of unbelief, with the corollary that contemporary unbelief was no special type of crisis but just another set of changes. Yet on the other hand, Bellah's notion of an emergent value consensus involved him in saying that we were all now tentative in our 'belief', Marxist, Christian and Rationalist alike: hence the emerging consensus of the uncertain was an emerging consensus of incipient unbelief. Having claimed that 'all believe something', Professor Bellah also claimed 'all disbelieve something'.

Henri de Lubac added some historical and philosophical points. From a philosophical viewpoint he saw no need to contrast cognition with subjectivity, at least in such a way that religion had no cognitive element. It was not necessary to identify all objective cognition with positive science, and therefore not necessary to eliminate the supposed clash of science and faith by dissolving faith in psychology, even depth psychology. Moreover, the OT specifically included a faith in 'facts' and the acts of God in history.

Thomas Luckmann's paper turned on a series of transitions. First there was a situation of 'primitive fusion' in which religious conduct, kinship behaviour and economic action were wedded in an indissoluble and unproblematic unity of meaning. This persisted from primitive society into the great archaic civilizations. Thereafter the social structure was gradually segmented into varied institutional domains, each achieving its own autonomy from the similarly specialized sphere of religion. The specialization of religious institutions and the variety of social strata in a given society led both to the standardization and systematization of an 'official' model of religion (theology) – more particularly so in Western Christendom – and to the elaboration of different versions within the various strata. At this point 'unbelief' in the sense of a divergent style and/or direct intellectual confrontation of the systematizations proposed by the sacred experts began to occur.

In the final stages of this process it may be that the social form of religion will begin to disappear and with it 'official' models or points of reference for determining what shall count as 'unbelief'. Indeed, in Europe the old religious beliefs have become marginal and in America penetrated by 'civic religion' as well as co-existing in a mutual plurality where each relativizes the other. Finally, perhaps, there arises a 'self-steered' religion where each person shops on an open market of religious possibilities albeit to some extent in accordance with his structural position in society. Some people no doubt retain the old ex-official model of religion in a naïve fashion, or retain it as a useful rhetoric on certain occasions without letting it too much disturb their private lives, or recover it in a highly personal way after a period of doubt and struggle. But for the sociologist a plurality of concrete religious institutions and complete subjective fragmentation mean that there is no means of determining what shall count as unbelief; indeed there are as many varied models of unbelief as there are models of socialization into which individuals may be inducted.[4]

To begin with the evolutionary scheme, the same criticism was made as of Bellah's scheme: stages may arise alongside each other without straightforward replacement. Another parallel criticism was advanced by Martin Marty to the effect that both Luckmann's notion of self-steered secondary socialization and Bellah's celebration of anti-authoritarianism as a growing theme overlooked the 'other-directedness' of modern society. It was also objected by Talcott Parsons that earlier stages *did* involve contradiction of the official system: the essential transition was from the heresy of that period to the unbelief of the present. In any case earlier stages also involved the confrontation of rival religions ('infidels') though Bryan Wilson thought it important that systematization, belief and therefore exclusiveness belonged largely to the Christian-Islamic group of religions. More broadly Houtart was against attempting to locate belief/unbelief either by choosing an 'official' point of departure or by dislocating belief/unbelief in the manner proposed by Luckmann. It was in his view more profitable to study the extent to which transitions might have occurred to an exclusively rational/ functional/technical frame of reference, to a loss of belief in a personal God, to a comparative weakening of magical notions concerning forces above mankind, and so on.

It was further argued that underlying Luckmann's scheme was the growth of freedom and individuation. David Martin suggested that this could be represented grammatically in the following way, taking into account the obvious difference which had been proposed between 'belief' and 'faith'. Supposing for example one took the following fundamental statements of faith and the religions to which they belong:

There is no God but God (Islam)
I believe in one God (Catholicism)
He has saved me, even me (Protestantism)

Each represents in turn an increasing element of the personal, from the impersonality of Islam, to the personal belief of Catholicism to the highly personal faith of Protestantism. Now, all of these contain a transcendental reference as well as a transition from 'One' to 'I' to 'Me'. The modern world, however, has seen both a radical extension of subjectivity and a radical rejection of it. Existentialism represents the pure Me with no object; it is in turn rejected by a revived Buddhism which also eliminates the subject itself.[5] On the other hand, Marxism reinstates the collective Us and finds, however, that this 'Us' of the proletarian brotherhood is always converted into the ubiquitous 'Them' of new forms of domination. The problem was therefore to study shifts from statements with transcendental reference to those without, as well as the 'growth of freedom'.

Samuel Klausner and Ivan Varga proposed another set of transitions. In their view it was possible to note all kinds of phenomena seemingly common to what was conventionally understood as religion and also outside it, such as dread, reverence, ritualization, conversion, rejection of the world, etc. These phenomena might have a varied social incidence, be more or less found together and interrelated, be to this or that extent institutionalized. This enabled one to move freely in one's investigations without needing to define belief and unbelief. It was at the same time possible and important to ask in what circumstances they occurred within a church and when they were specifically in relation to God: conversion to God, ritualization of divine worship, dread of God, rejections of the world based on a transcendent perspective and so on.[6]

The third set of controversies also involved an American–European contrast, not this time in terms of a preference for or against taking 'official' religion and institutions as convenient starting-points, but in terms of degrees of pessimism and the amount of emphasis placed on empirical, especially survey, research. With regard to the last, Charles Glock presented a very interesting set of proposals which were, however, not specially problematic. Bryan Wilson replying to this paper plainly felt that long-term institutional analysis enabled one to deal with specific cultural configurations in a way head-counting did not. He was for a different style of empiricism, with a longer historical perspective than the survey. More important than this, however, he presented his material within an overall pessimistic frame, particularly with respect to the supposed growth of freedom, and so brought about a conflict with the more optimistic frame of Talcott Parsons.

Basically Wilson pointed to a set of changes which affected society as a whole and of which the troubles experienced by religious institutions were but one aspect. These changes were set in motion by the dominance of a machine culture and a rationalized bureaucracy able to erode the communal, the affective and intimate, and to attenuate authentic experience. Religion was essentially linked to these, either through the local parish of a church or the small sectarian group. The disappearance of religion approximated the disappearance of community. Moreover, the old style of community required a personal, familial style of legitimation, while bureaucracy only required a pragmatic sanction in terms of certain broad social aims. As bureaucratic styles expand so machines increasingly govern our life and dictate its basic assumptions, leaving beliefs as a marginal, vestigial private luxury, albeit still achieving some objective specification in the churches. Indeed, even private life was now increasingly dominated by machines, and people were enabled to block out religious questions in all except moments of personal anguish.

The changing situation of the office worker might provide an example. Previously the office worker performed his tasks within a texture of personal relations and he received intimations of culture from above. Now, however, office technology, data processing, the increasing size and rationality of the 'bureau' reduce human involvements in the course of work, eliminate nuances, sensitivities, and the moral imperatives and personal integrity associated with them. Moreover, such a process could have implications for the viability of supernatural beliefs, especially those couched in human terms. It was not easy to see how Christianity could reinterpret itself to deal with these changes.[7]

In a broader context we should look at the nature of the new élites who controlled the new technology, especially the mass media, in particular their capacity to batten on the intelligentsia for ideas, their substitution of technical for rhetorical skills, and their ability through the media to dominate leisure in such a way as to achieve a near-permanent deflection from religious concerns. Indeed, the unstructured field of leisure, once so despised, was now a Cinderella come to the Ball.[8] In sum, the common cultural style and worldview of both preacher and humanist, rooted in personal sensitivity, literacy and extended rhetoric was threatened by the packaged immediacy and the conspicuous trivialization purveyed by mass communications technology.[9]

Talcott Parsons protested that Wilson's analysis of the machine age always verged on viewing the world as 'dominated' by technology rather than as 'conditioned' by it. Technology conditioned us in the same sense as did our biological equipment. He thought it curious that all the advances of the past three centuries were originally perceived as restrictions on freedom when they were ultimately extensions of self-determination. In the seventeenth century science showed that God did not sustain the universe by free individual decisions; in the nineteenth century it showed that God did not make man by a sovereign act of creation; now sociology and psychology show that we do not even make ourselves. Yet each realization

of new determinisms and of lawfulness created parallel possibilities
of exploiting such realization in the interests of new freedoms.

The final set of issues turned around the contemporary processes of
birth, primary socialization, secondary socialization and death.
Each of these was seen as having implications for religious awareness.
Peter Berger introduced these themes and they were somewhat
elaborated by Talcott Parsons. Berger pointed to the qualitative
difference in the experience of childhood, the growth of a 'sensitivity culture' as a means of secondary socialization and the way in
which death has become invisible, 'bracketed in consciousness'.
Childhood is now simply happier than it ever was, both as a continuing experience and because on the average children no longer die
nor experience the death of their parents. The changed role of
parents has implications for the perception of all authority, metaphysical authority included, just as generally 'happy' youthful perception of the world has implications for metaphysics in general.
Such a perception makes them radically incapable of coping with
the world when eventually exposed to it, and arouses in them a
demand for the humanization of the world which is bound to be
partially frustrated. Moreover, in their new exposed position they
encounter quite contrary tendencies: on the one hand the war in
Vietnam, or blueprints for eliminating fifty million people at the
press of a button, on the other the fact that 1968 was the first year in
which there were no executions in the United States.[10]
   Talcott Parsons amplified this, arguing that the invisibility of
death occurred both because of medical advances and the erosion
of the extended network of kin. Because death involves less suffering
it raises less potent questions of meaning, and death after full
maturity becomes non-tragic.[11] In any case the special psychological
maturity derived from the experiences of death now comes later in
life. Religion has a special concern with experiences of birth and
death, and the Christian religion in particular turns on the redemp-
tive birth and sacrificial death of Christ. All these changes in human
experience cannot but affect the salience which these key events for
religion continue to have in our experience. Its central symbols
become relevant in a highly intermittent way, particularly so when
(as Wilson argued) a continuing community has dissolved and when
social policies no longer need invoke religious sanction. In short,
religion is placed at one or two removes away from almost all our

immediate concerns. This is a central development lying behind the culture of unbelief – or in Wilson's terms, the culture of apathy and neglect.

NOTES

1. Inevitably there were discussions of what was meant by 'transcendental', in particular with regard to 'mundane transcendence' such as occurs in LSD experiences or, quite differently, in the concepts of transcendence used by contemporary Marxists.

2. As one comment put it: 'The death of the God of cognitive explanation is followed by the death of the God of social legitimation.'

3. In my own view the end of 'total theology' complements the concept of the end of 'total ideology' and the supposed emergent value consensus is centred – not in the medieval village – but in the 'Electronic Village' of communications technology.

4. In my view such an analysis presents a purely logical point: that if you define belief by official system X then unbelief will be Y, whereas if you define it as any of the systems of personal relevance a, b, c into which a person may be socially inducted then unbeliefs are defined in any number of ways p, q, r. But the logical point, though it does not require any evolutionary scheme, is in fact linked by Luckmann to just such a scheme. Moreover it raises questions as to which of the varied religious organizations or purely personal 'systems of relevance' fit this or that milieu of modern society and how far these alternatives really are 'functional equivalents' one of the other.

5. I retain a sharp recollection of the student who suddenly announced in a tutorial that he had 'gone beyond Existentialism'. When I asked what that meant he replied, 'Zen'.

6. Ivan Varga also suggested *en passant* that with secular life increasingly organized in accordance with canons of functional rationality these phenomena (dread, etc.) were resistant to incorporation in any structure which was as organized and comparatively systematic as a church.

7. Harvey Cox's *The Secular City* is one such attempt: one which Bryan Wilson would presumably deplore. Unfortunately the absence of Harvey Cox at this juncture prevented a confrontation between pessimistic 'non-believer' and optimistic 'believer'.

8. Cf. William Pickering, 'Religion – a Leisure-time Pursuit?' in D. Martin (ed.), *A Sociological Yearbook of Religion in Britain 1*, SCM Press 1968.

9. An engaging illustration of this was provided for me at a meeting of the Methodist Education Committee where the attack of the technical college representatives drew together both ministers and university teachers, just as the forward thrust of mass society, technology and bureaucratic administration often draws together the religious believer and the university student. Yet it was interesting that in the British context at least the protagonists of the technical colleges were anxious to show that they too held liberal notions of education and were not 'rude mechanicks'.

10. And if one may add a felicitous statistic for Britain: not a single soldier killed on active service in 1968.

11. Perhaps one ought to think of the highly distasteful implications of 'Immortality Inc.' as presented by Alan Whicker.

2 Some Aspects of Religious Life in an Immigrant Area in Manchester

Robin H. Ward

THE decline in the practice of religion on the part of the urban working class in Britain is a familiar process.[1] What has been less well documented,[2] is the consequences for church life of a large number of immigrants, with a much higher rate of churchgoing before coming to England, becoming residents in such a working-class area characterized by declining churchgoing. This article considers some evidence about the consequences of the movement of Irish and coloured, mainly West Indian, immigrants into Moss Side, Manchester; it also suggests some of the factors which will determine the response of the existing churches to such arrivals and the ways in which the immigrants adapt to such a situation.

The data to be analysed come from a random sample survey of 765 residents in Moss Side and two adjacent districts with a somewhat higher status, Victoria Park and Whalley Range.[3] Particular attention is given to information on the religious behaviour and attitudes of 275 West Indians included in this sample, almost all living in Moss Side. This has been supplemented by discussions with the clergy of churches in Moss Side and participant observation in some of the churches, particularly Seventh Day Adventist and Pentecostal.

The Socio-economic characteristics of Moss Side

Moss Side is not and never has been a 'traditional' working-class area. Originally built towards the end of the nineteenth century for the upper-middle class and the superior working class who were involved in the industrial expansion of Manchester, it lost much of its population during the inter-war years: the merchants and managers, no longer able to afford personal service to keep up their rambling properties, were attracted to the new private suburbia outside Manchester which through improvements in transport now gave easier access to the city; they were followed by the artisans who abandoned Moss Side in favour of suburban council estates such as Wythenshawe.[4]

They were replaced by a succession of immigrant groups: Irish, African, European, West Indian and Asian. But in addition the low rents attracted many newly-formed English households; and the anonymity of life in the lodging houses into which the merchants' dwellings had been turned drew a variety of people living on the fringes of respectable society. Moss Side became, in fact, in many ways a zone of transition comparable to that depicted by Rex and Moore in their study of Sparkbrook, Birmingham. It included the same five categories of residents: the old-established white population; newly-formed white households; white social misfits; single, temporary migrants; and immigrant families whose residence had become more permanent. In three ways, however, all related to the housing market (Rex and Moore emphasize that this is the crucial determinant of life in such an area), Moss Side appears to be different from Sparkbrook:

1. A larger supply of reasonably cheap accommodation to buy is available outside Moss Side. Thus, the inclination of immigrant families for house-ownership has in many cases been satisfied. Usually the areas they have chosen are near enough to Moss Side to enable them to continue to shop there, and to keep up their church affiliations and social contacts.

2. In addition, immigrant families have increasingly turned to council accommodation to solve their housing problems. In contrast to Sparkbrook, more than two hundred coloured families from Moss Side have been given council tenancies through the waiting list, many in nearby Hulme. In this way, too, many who by their initiative have moved out of Moss Side and bettered their housing situation still look to it for the satisfaction of their religious needs.

3. The exodus particularly of white families from Moss Side has been accelerated by the threat of redevelopment which has hovered over the area for some years. Many houses in Moss Side are not only unfashionable: they are about to be condemned, and in consequence even more of the white residents who formed the nucleus of the local churches have moved to other districts.

Before examining the consequences of such factors for churches in Moss Side, we must understand the religious background of immigrants who have come to reside there.

Religious background of immigrants to Moss Side

Two basic dimensions of a man's religious situation are the denomination he belongs to and the importance he attaches to religion. We shall look at these in turn. To begin with, very few from any country claimed to have no religion. In this the immigrants resembled the local-born population, many of whom stated that they rarely, if ever, went to church, but they still belonged to a particular denomination and felt that religion was important to them.

Secondly, the religious adherence of most of the immigrants could be predicted once their countries of origin were known. Thus, the Irish and Europeans (mainly refugees from Poland or migrant workers from Southern Europe) were almost entirely Roman Catholic. The Asians, except for a number of Sikh families clustered round their temple, were Muslim. The Africans also included a number of Muslims from Nigeria as well as Anglicans and Roman Catholics. There was most diversity among the West Indians: the main groups were Anglican, Roman Catholic, Methodist, Baptist, Pentecostal, Church of God, and Seventh Day Adventist.

The pattern of church allegiance of men and women was almost identical. The two significant exceptions were that more of the English women were Church of England; and that more West Indian women were Anglican while the men were more likely to be Roman Catholics.

Turning more specifically to the West Indians, we can see that their religious affiliation depends to a large extent on which islands have provided the most immigrants. Most cities in Britain with West Indians have Jamaicans and Leeward Islanders and Barbadians and Trinidadians, but in greatly varying proportions. What is distinctive is that the status system derived from the islands tends to reproduce itself in Britain and is reflected in the partial segregation of communities from the different islands. Thus in Manchester the main area of residence of 'small islanders' is within Moss Side. But few Barbadians or Trinidadians live there. And it is only one of the districts where Jamaicans predominate. Thus the Jamaicans in Moss Side provide most of the Baptists, many of the Anglicans, and a large majority of the Adventists, Pentecostalists and members of the Church of God. The Leeward Islanders, especially Kitticians, are frequently Methodist (the local Methodist church is the base for the Leeward Islands People's Association). There are few West Indian Roman

Catholics, and those that do live in Moss Side are not on the whole from Roman Catholic islands such as Trinidad (Trinidadians live in more desirable residential areas, commensurate with their socio-economic status), but Jamaican men from Kingston.

Informants were asked how important religion was to them and the answers were classified as 'very important', 'important', 'not very important' or 'not important at all'. Pakistanis were most likely to regard their religion as very important, followed by Africans, Irish and Europeans, and West Indians, with the white English population least likely to regard religion as important.

There was also a significant variation between Moss Side itself and Victoria Park and Whalley Range. Almost half of those in the two latter districts stated that religion was very important to them and less than one-tenth regarded it as not important at all. In Moss Side, however, only one-quarter said it was very important, and twice as many as in the other districts gave it no importance.

It is interesting to examine where this difference lay. It was not among the Irish, who tended to regard religion as very important wherever they lived. Nor was it due to the Pentecostalists and Adventists (those who have bettered themselves while living in Moss Side, whether as a result of their Protestant ethic or not, have moved out not to Whalley Range or Victoria Park, but to other districts where more suitable bought accommodation was available). To some extent the variation found was due to the Pakistanis, who tended to live outside Moss Side. Substantially, however, we found that it was the English population and the Protestants from the West Indies and Africa who were more likely to say that religion was of great importance if they lived in the more desirable areas of Victoria Park and Whalley Range. One interesting feature of this is that almost all respondents who said that religion used to be important, but was not now, lived in Moss Side. That is, they were not people who had through the ethical demands of their religion been able to move to more pleasant surroundings and subsequently lost their fervour: they had come to Moss Side regarding religion as important but had since felt this importance wane.

Finally, we may note that church allegiance and estimates of the importance of religion are closely associated: Muslims, Roman Catholics, Adventists, Pentecostalists and Church of God tended to regard their religion as very important; Anglicans frequently regarded it as unimportant; Methodists and Baptists came in between.

Patterns of church attendance in Moss Side

It is convenient before examining the pattern of churchgoing in Moss Side to review briefly the existing provision of churches in the area. Most of them were built some decades before coloured families came to live in Moss Side to serve a very different community.

Five of these churches are Anglican, two Methodist and one Baptist. In addition there are two Roman Catholic churches, catering especially for Polish and Irish residents, and a Roman Catholic mission; a Congregational church and a Church of Christ, a flourishing, originally-white Pentecostal church and two Spiritualist churches. Probably as many churches, however, have been started since the arrival of West Indians to the area.[5] These fall within the Pentecostal–Church of God cluster, and are mainly direct off-shoots of established American churches, such as the New Testament Church of God, or after an early phase of independence have negotiated some form of sponsorship with an American body, such as the Bethel United Church of Jesus Christ Apostolic with the Church of God in Christ of Baltimore. Typically in the first stage the church meets in the home of one of the members; subsequently, arrangements are made to book a room in a local school or other suitable building; in the final stage, money is raised to buy a redundant building from a conventional denomination or, latterly, to apply for a site to build a new church on the neighbouring council estate of Hulme. The economic benefits arising from sponsorship enable this process to be achieved more quickly. There are also religious groups which do not have premises within Moss Side, so that residents move out of the area on Sunday (or Saturday) for their worship. These include Jehovah's Witnesses and, most importantly, Seventh Day Adventists.

We now examine attendance at those churches.[6] The eight Anglican, Methodist and Baptist churches had an average weekly church attendance (including Sunday School) of about 1,200. Just over 500 of these, or rather less than half, were coloured, all but 40 of them being West Indians. Adults formed only slightly more than half of this number, but there was a very significant difference in this between white and coloured attenders, which suggests a point to be developed later, that they are present at different stages of the life cycle and have different interests which may feed into the roles that are allocated within the context of the activities of the church. Thus more than two-thirds of the white church-attenders were adults, compared with less than one-third of the coloured. The Baptist minister, for instance, when asked for general comments on the situation of immigrants in his church, stressed the difficulty of white and coloured making contact: while the white congregation tended to be elderly, the West Indians were much younger and had different working hours; they also had young families, which restricted their free time. The important thing was that this difference coincided with the colour line.

The same pattern is noticeable at the other white churches to which immigrants have become attached: at the Pentecostal church, about one-third of the congregation are coloured – it was much more until the New Testament Church of God acquired their own church buildings just down the road; the Seventh Day Adventists, partly through the tithes produced by a very effective evangelistic campaign, were able to build a new church, and again an ageing white population was invigorated by a large number of Jamaicans – on a normal Sabbath possibly 150 out of 250 present are coloured.

In all these churches, however, whether located within Moss Side or not, a large proportion of the congregation is not resident within Moss Side. Many of the white churchgoers today are former residents who commute back to the area for their Sunday worship and serve as a reminder of its previous days. Indeed, although the level of church attendance of West Indians living in Moss Side is low, that of the local white residents, with the exception of the Irish Roman Catholics, is much lower.

Figures from the sample survey, to which we now return, only refer to people living in the three areas covered. These show that six churches, all of them previously white denominations, had the allegiance of more than 2% of the West Indians interviewed. Together they accounted for rather more than one-third of the respondents. While the greatest number spoke of Anglican churches, the most popular single church was the Baptist church, which was mentioned by 29 out of 275.

Personal experience suggests that if surrounding areas such as Rusholme and Old Trafford had been sampled, the proportion of West Indian Pentecostalists would have been much greater. Indeed, our own calculations are that at least as many West Indians attend Pentecostal and Church of God churches in and around Moss Side as all the other denominations together, with the Seventh Day Adventists excepted.

To summarize, Roman Catholics were frequent churchgoers, and Anglicans infrequent, with Methodists and Baptists coming in between. But the Muslims, the Adventists and the Pentecostal and Church of God groups were polarized into those who were very regular in their attendance and those who never went to church or mosque at all. This was particularly true of the Pentecostalists: while they were all inclined to stress the importance of their religion, they were split into those who played an integral part in the life of a frequently small and intimate church, and those for whom church-going no longer had any relevance.

Church attendance is not the only criterion of affiliation, and it may under-estimate the extent of felt allegiance. The Anglican clergyman who only has an average of 40 immigrants in his church on Sunday has still performed 650 coloured baptisms within the last seven years. But it must be taken to indicate a measure of decline. Whereas 116 of the 275 interviewed claimed to have been frequent church attenders at home (a minority even then), only 20 claimed this now; and while 27 said that their church attendance was infrequent at home, 110 gave this reply when speaking of the present.[7]

The data do not suggest, then, a complete failure of participation in church life: some never went to church even in the West Indies; some have stopped going since arriving in England, some have been incorporated into white churches; and some have formed their own bodies. In the rest of the paper we examine factors which may help to account for the variation in the success of the churches and the reactions of immigrants. These are (i) demographic aspects, (ii) theological emphasis and type of mission, (iii) socio-economic factors, (iv) organization, (v) the different functions which churches come to perform.

Factors affecting the attractiveness of churches to immigrants

(i) Demographic aspects

Sociologists have frequently noted the correlation of churchgoing and other religious behaviour with demographic aspects of the population under scrutiny. That is, they have noted a tendency for church attendance to be associated with a particular age group, sex and marital status. There is, of course, no mechanical process whereby young married people, for example, are less likely to attend church than the retired. But it is certainly true that at certain stages in the life cycle there are pressures and interests which make church attendance more or less likely. The point we are making in this section is that the demographic composition of immigrants in Moss Side is such that they are less likely to be active in church life than white residents.

For our first example we may simply note that in all social classes women tend to be over-represented in churches. But among practically all immigrant groups, the proportion of men to women is much larger than in the receiving population. Thus while 10 % of West Indian households in Moss Side consisted only of a woman and children, there were still more West Indian men than women overall. The same was true for the Asians, Irish and other immigrant groups.

We may consider in more detail a second demographic factor, that of age. The sample survey showed a predictable trend towards a higher level of churchgoing, the older the population. Thus Roman Catholics were regular church-attenders at all ages, but still somewhat less frequent in the 21–40 age group. The Anglicans were infrequent attenders at all ages, but even more infrequent at ages 21–30. Methodists again were infrequent attenders in this age range. Interestingly, exactly the same was found among the Muslims: half of those aged 21–30 went to mosque infrequently, compared with one-third of those aged 31–40 and none of those older than 40.

The importance of this is seen when we compare the age range of the English and coloured samples. Less than half of the English were aged 21–40, as against more than two-thirds of the coloured, mainly West Indian, sample. At the other extreme, while more than one-quarter of the English were aged 60 and above, only one in fifty of the coloured group were of this age.

We conclude that immigrants are in the age and sex categories which among the white population have the lowest rate of church attendance. With some over-simplification, churches in Moss Side could be described as consisting of five categories: (i) elderly English people (aged 55 and above), (ii) adult West Indians (aged 30–55), (iii) young adult English (aged 20–30), (iv) teenagers, mainly West Indian (aged 14–20), (v) younger children, again the majority coloured (aged 0–14). Only children in category five seem to show a substantial overlap between white and coloured.

It would require more intensive research to spell out the implications for particular churches of this distribution. All we can do here is to suggest that on a demographic basis immigrants are particularly vulnerable to the pressures which lower rates of church attendance among the host population. It remains to be seen whether this will be affected when the age range of immigrant groups approximates more closely to that in which church attendance is more likely. For with the passage of time immigrants will not only become older, and hence more likely to engage in church activities, especially with their typically active religious background; they will also become more acculturated to a way of life in which churchgoing has no part. It is dangerous to predict the future religious behaviour of recent immigrants by examining the present situation of those who have been here longer. It is interesting to note, however, that among both the Irish and the Africans, those who came to England before 1955 regard religion as less important, despite being substantially older. Among the West Indians, however, those who immigrated before 1955 include to a striking degree both those who regard religion as not important at all and those who see it as very important. It is the most recent immigrants who have more moderate views on religion. We might hypothesize from this that those who came to Britain from an active church background are likely to take one of two courses: if they become closely attached to a church which can provide a buffer against the secularizing influences of the outside society, as they grow older they are more likely to feel the increasing attachment to religion which is characteristic of the older age groups; if they do not have this stable organizational base, acculturation is likely to include a decreasing attachment to religion. Those who have arrived most recently have not yet been exposed to English society for long enough for their attachment to their religion to be polarized in either direction.

A fuller discussion of this would mean examining the range of socio-economic influences to which immigrants are likely to be exposed, both within and outside the church. First, however, we should look briefly at the theological emphases of the churches themselves, to see in what ways socio-economic factors are likely to become relevant.

(ii) *Theology and mission*

Churches have often been contrasted on the basis of whether their theological emphases have stressed that the worldly success of their members is legitimate in the sight of God, or whether their religious status within the church compensates for their lack of achievement in the world around them. We need hardly add that the current emphasis in a particular church need not coincide with its received theology. Indeed in predicting the growth of respectability of the Methodist Church, Wesley was only anticipating some of the more recent descriptions of the circumstances in which sects which took root among the disprivileged have become respectable middle-class denominations.[8]

The point we are concerned with here is that wherever on the continuum of respectability particular churches are placed, they will attract people from particular social backgrounds with particular types of life experience. The conventional denominations will all, in fact, whether consciously or not, emphasize the legitimacy of the life situations of the typical white members; they have achieved something in their lives, and driving back to church in Moss Side on Sunday only serves to confirm this.

Most of the West Indians, too, have come from churches which legitimated the success and the status they enjoyed in the islands. But the slightly paler skin shade or the skilled job which earned a man respect in Jamaica are not likely to carry so much weight in Britain. Apprenticeship regulations may have denied him access to his trade, and to white people black is black, whatever the shade. There are two consequences: his total life situation is not likely to be one in which he is looking for achievements in British society to be legitimated; and even if he were, English congregations in areas whose loss of respectability can easily be put down to the incursion of coloured families are only likely to accept him as of an equal status if he is the individual whom, through personal acquaintance, they have found to be the exception to the prevalent stereotype. Conveniently, theological emphases, in so far as they are communicated at all, are not spelled out in terms which apply the basic implications of an egalitarian gospel to the life situation of the members. Thus while Moberg, speaking of the USA, can point out that 'concepts of social justice basic in the struggle for Negro rights have come largely from religion' (and in Britain, too, at a national level, churches have pushed towards liberal policies in race relations), he also confirms that 'ethnocentrism has been linked with religious identifications throughout history' and that 'churches may accentuate and reinforce attitudes of antipathy toward other groups'.[9]

(iii) *Socio-economic aspects*

We have suggested that the theological emphasis of a particular church will lead to a degree of selection among its members. Again, the typical socio-economic profiles of its members will give it an image which reinforces its attraction to some and lack of attraction to others. That is, the church does not just consist of saved (or unsaved) people; its members have distinctive interests, attitudes, and social backgrounds, and its attractiveness to newcomers will depend partly on their compatibility with this.

In terms of occupational levels, the sample from Moss Side, Victoria Park and Whalley Range are predominantly manual workers, with some routine non-manual employees and only 10% in the Registrar General's social classes I and II (most of those, except for the West Indian nurses, being resident in Victoria Park and Whalley Range). Denominations and particular churches varied considerably in the typical social class (i.e. occupational status) of their members. Thus Roman Catholics and Anglicans were equally distributed among non-manual, skilled, semi-skilled and unskilled manual groups. Among the Methodists, however, there was a tendency for the men to be clerical workers or skilled manual, while their wives were more often doing semi-skilled work, particularly machine-operating in the engineering and clothing trades. The Pentecostalists were even more homogeneous, both men and women being typically in social class three.

It is undoubtedly true that white and coloured within Moss Side do not differ significantly in their occupational background. For both, the socio-economic groups most likely to be attending churches are heavily under-represented. But we have already stated that the local white population is even less churched than the immigrants. The white nuclei of the Moss Side churches, in fact, tend to come from outside the area, and their occupational distribution is substantially higher than that of Moss Siders, white or coloured. Thus, within the context of the churches, there is often an important difference in the social class of white and coloured.

More important than the difference in typical occupations, however, is the fact that it frequently coincides with the difference in status between white and black in the same congregation. Indeed, aspects of status quite unrelated to skin colour are of considerable importance. Baptists and Methodists will frequently look on

Pentecostalists with scorn, whether or not they happen to have lower status occupations. But differences of status due to skin colour are more pervasive. Whatever the social and occupational background of West Indians in Moss Side, in most social contexts black means inferior, and white congregations, particularly in view of their association with the Moss Side of the past, need a powerful ideology to enable them to overcome this feeling. What can easily happen is what Rex and Moore observed in an Anglican church in Sparkbrook: it was the non-churchgoing parishioners who felt the greatest resentment against the West Indians in the congregation; the vicar was theirs, and he should be looking after them rather than 'fraternizing with coloured people'.[10] That is, differences in the degree of commitment to Christian values will affect attitudes to coloured arrivals.

Of course churches may be, and often are, more effective than other organizations in uniting people from different occupational backgrounds and with different statuses. But these differences of status are a very real factor in structuring relations between black and white in a local congregation. To some extent all churches come to uphold and symbolize a particular set of cultural values, as well as providing a system of beliefs. The success a particular church enjoys in integrating white and black is likely to be related to how influential the potentially unifying beliefs are in cushioning an affront to the style of life of the white congregation when coloured Christians come into the church.

We can in any case expect some coloured families to opt out of churchgoing altogether. Coming from a high status background in the West Indies to a position of disprivilege in Moss Side, they can either join a respectable white church which is unlikely to accept them fully, and which legitimates a style of life they do not fully share, or they can become attached to a low status, probably West Indian church, which they had previously looked down on, but which will provide support against and compensation for the damage to their self-image which they suffer in British society. In face of this it may be surprising that the white denominations have received so many West Indians into their churches.

(iv) *Organization and church order*

Churches differ substantially in the range of activities available and the way these are organized. This is partly a consequence of their

B

concepts of mission and church order. But it will also reflect the socio-economic status of their members. Different types of activities flow from particular emphases on ritual and pageantry, emotional experiences or the satisfaction of intellectual capacities. In each case the activities of the church involve a range of official positions, each with its own role attached, and more generally a range of situations in which the behaviour is structured according to the theology, traditions and culture of the church.

To some extent the traditions of the church will express the social origins of past members. All churches have a programme which in some ways reflects the style of life of their members as well as the theology of the denomination. This is not a bad thing, because churchmen would argue that the work of the church consisted in applying the gospel to the particular circumstances of the members rather than theological abstractions. What we are suggesting, however, is that churches will differ in the extent to which 'the outside gets in'; that is, in the importance of roles played outside the church in structuring behaviour within the church.

Conversely, the more pervasive the beliefs of the church, and the more extensive the roles which are structured in accordance with these beliefs and with the recognized policy of the church which springs from the beliefs, the more likely it is that harmonious relations can develop between white and black which are not based on the unequal statuses these groups carry in the wider society.

Thus, in the conduct of worship, the more scope there is for individuals and groups to participate according to a pattern which is publicly recognized in the church, for example in prayers, readings, musical contributions and other 'items', the more the likelihood of equality of status and hence of treatment inside the church. Naturally, where the important jobs are as a matter of course given to white members, and coloured members are only allocated simple duties which require no responsibility, this image can easily be perpetuated. Interviews with clergy and observation in churches in Moss Side suggest that this may be an important factor, and that quite apart from the number of roles available for coloured members to fill, the attitude of the clergyman and the lay readers to colour may be crucial in defining which of them can be occupied by immigrants.

We may take as a second example youth organizations within a church. There is some evidence that coloured teenagers can be integrated more effectively within a youth organization where the behaviour is highly structured, particularly within uniformed organizations, where the uniform is just one aspect of the way in which roles and behaviour are defined by the organization, not by the individual members. By way of contrast, we should expect that the more 'free' the activities within a youth club, the more they would reflect attitudes to colour derived from outside.

There is a limit, however, to what individual churches can do about this factor. For example, a Methodist church which copied the enthusiastic services of Pentecostalism, because it allowed more scope for 'participation', would be more likely to alienate both its white members and the West Indian Methodists, who are probably used to a liturgical service on Sunday. Where the minister and leaders can act, however, is in constantly working to expand the range of offices filled by immigrants, and being prepared to do a certain amount of 'nursing' in the process. But they should recognize that this may not be to the liking of the white members. More than once, in fact, a key white member has admitted that he returns to church in Moss Side on Sunday because he knows he can 'rule the roost' there, while he feels he could not cope with the middle-class church in his present area of residence. For such reasons a radical redistribution of offices could run into strong opposition. We may recall the regretful comment of one clergyman who had been working in Moss Side for some years, who declared that his attempts to win over his congregation gradually to the implications of being a multiracial church had failed, and that his best course would have been to get tough earlier on, whatever the consequences. These are bold words, but when the clergyman's tenure of office is as precarious as it is in some denominations, one can understand a policy of caution.

Again, the expectations which English and West Indian members have about appropriate organizational structure and leadership styles within the church can differ greatly. Typically, in an English church, offices are seen as a functional way of ensuring that a minimum of people are responsible for a maximum of duties. On the other hand, West Indians may feel that almost all those who comprise the church should have some official position. There are different expectations, too, as to how offices should be carried out. West Indians expect clearly defined roles, structured activities (such as uniformed organizations) and formal teaching of children. Two churches in Moss Side which retain a rather pedagogic Sunday School system have almost entirely West Indian classes. Another church which has stressed the use of free methods in teaching has many fewer West Indians enrolled; some indeed have been withdrawn because it was not formal enough: children were going there to play (as they did to English day schools). But the West Indians with leadership qualities who could help direct activities according to such expectations are not regularly available because of their family situation and the exigencies of shift work. Even the role the minister is expected to play may be viewed differently. English families may have come to realize the wider role he plays because of his concern for their total lives within the community. But the West Indians are likely to regard any clergyman who departs from a traditional pastoral ministry with deep suspicion.

The two previously-white churches which have integrated coloured families most effectively into all levels of the organization are the Pentecostal and the Seventh Day Adventist churches, which are both outside Moss Side. The Adventist church is indeed quite fashionably situated next to a synagogue and well away from the areas with the highest proportion of immigrants. Many of the West Indians who attend, in fact, also live in other parts of Manchester, though some have moved there from Moss Side. Coloured members form a majority in the church, many of them from high-status occupations, particularly nurses. Here is a church of rising status and influence, belonging to a sect which is coming closer to the conventional denominations, but which still imposes a severe ethic on its members, who are expected to tithe their income, abstain from tea and coffee as well as alcohol, and do no work on the Sabbath, as well as working systematically for the church in a wide range of activities. The transformation of a declining and ageing white congregation into a large and effectively multi-racial body has not been automatic. In many places Seventh Day Adventists have experienced difficulties in this process. In this case, however, while the distribution of offices is skewed towards white members having the most responsible posts, integration has undoubtedly been effective. Here above all, white and coloured interact with each other in a wide range of contexts, all of them part of the church's programme of devotional, educational and social service activities.

(v) *Functional aspects*

We have already suggested that though a church is established for religious purposes, it is likely to acquire other functions, intended or unintended, more or less directly related to its original programme. We do not propose to discuss whether or not these functions are 'religious'. All we are concerned to do in this final section is to examine briefly the functions which churches in immigrant areas seem likely to fulfil. We shall imply that in so far as they are able to acquire these functions, they are more likely to attract coloured newcomers to the area into the life of the church.

Rex and Moore speak of five positive functions which the churches in Sparkbrook perform:

(i) They provide comfort and security to the old and bewildered. Glock and Stark suggest that in the USA it is not only the old and bewildered who are in churches because they seek the comforts of the faith, but the most active Christian lay people on whose participation and resources the whole structure of the churches rests.[11] This seems likely to apply equally to churches in areas such as Moss Side.

(ii) They serve as welfare agencies which operate between the various statutory services offered in the Welfare State. In some areas where these have been formalized into 'advice centres' they have proved their value, although there are considerable difficulties in bridging the gap between the potential donors and recipients of advice. Even where such advice centres have been started with immigrants in mind, the local white population may in fact constitute the largest source of enquiries.

(iii) Some of the sects provide a suitable context for tension release among the more deprived sections of the immigrant population and give a meaning to their deprivation. We should qualify this judgment on the basis of our experience in Moss Side. Those who take a regular part in West Indian Pentecostal churches need not be among the most deprived: many have high status jobs, though this may itself involve them in more situations where they are deprived of the status their occupation would lead them to expect.

(iv) They encourage thrift and personal virtue, desirable properties in a hazardous urban environment. More specifically, they initially provide an ethic and a set of values which enables people to compensate for their disprivilege. Subsequently they provide the necessary conditions for immigrants to escalate out of Moss Side and find a more secure residential base.

(v) They make it possible for particular social and cultural groupings to assert their identity, replacing kin and friends who have not come to England. Thus within the same denomination one church will tend to attract Leeward Islanders, another Jamaicans, and another Barbadians.

Significantly, Rex and Moore do not claim that the churches in Sparkbrook function to challenge the members to respond to the great moral issues affecting society, such as poverty and race. In the choice between trying to run a successful organization and to awaken a congregation to face their responsibilities on current social issues, all the pressures of the situation induce the clergy to play safe. Theoretically this need not be a choice: security and challenge are equally intrinsic to the Christian gospel. But empirically there is a gulf between the two as wide as that described by Glock and Stark.[12] On the one side are the great majority whose prejudices are buttressed by their interpretations of the faith, comfort-seekers whose solution for the problems of society is massive individual transformation through Christ. On the other side are the restless minority, committed to Christian ethics, including racial justice, but much less closely involved in the administration of the church. The clergy attempt to straddle the gap. They may make valiant attempts at moral leadership, but normally they settle for a more orthodox ministry, concentrating on the individual religious needs of the members while envying fellow clergy in less exposed positions (such as theological colleges or universities) who are free to express the moral dilemmas that the parish clergy appreciate only too well, but dare not act on.

Conclusion

We have given some evidence of the situation of immigrant groups, particularly West Indians, within Moss Side, offered some preliminary interpretations and suggested hypotheses which might be tested. We have concentrated on the qualities of West Indians as immigrants (being newcomers, facing a precarious environment) and as coloured (having a low status ascribed to them, facing the possibility of rejection within and outside the church). What was also clear, however, was that they share a common class situation with white residents in Moss Side. Acculturation for them means moving into a common class culture, despite the hazards of their colour. We may expect indeed that the fact of the common class situation would make some kind of accommodation between white and black more likely. However, we should remember that the class whose culture immigrants are acquiring has long given up the practice of church-going. If, then, we are to address ourselves adequately to the question why immigrants have to a considerable extent ceased from religious practice, and how fuller participation within the churches should be planned, inevitably we are asking the broader question why has the English working class stopped going to church (or, in the light of Wickham's study, did they ever)?[13] To a large degree the churches' record of failure in integrating coloured newcomers into their congregations is simply part of their wider failure in integrating the white working class.

NOTES

1. See, for example, E. R. Wickham, *Church and People in an Industrial City*, Lutterworth Press 1957, which documents the process for Sheffield. I am grateful to Chris Pickvance, Gerry Wheale and Brian Jackson for their valuable comments on a draft of this article.

2. An exception is 'Religion in Sparkbrook', Chapter 7 in J. Rex and R. Moore, *Race, Community and Conflict*, OUP for the Institute of Race Relations 1967.

3. Financial support for this survey was provided by the Joseph Rowntree Memorial Trust and the National Institute of Economic and Social Research. Interviews were carried out in 1966–67.

4. The centrifugal aspects of the status system of urban housing are well described in Rex and Moore, op. cit.

5. For a full description of this process see M. J. C. Calley, *God's People: West Indian Pentecostal Sects in England*, OUP 1965.

6. Information given in this section on church attendances comes from interviews with the clergy and officials of these churches carried out in 1967, supplemented by informal participation.

7. 'Frequent' church attendance was defined as more than once a fortnight; 'infrequent' attendance was less than once every two months.

8. For a classical account see H. R. Niebuhr, *The Social Sources of Denominationalism*, Shoestring Press, Hamden, Conn. 1954.

9. D. A. Moberg, *The Church as a Social Institution*, Prentice-Hall, Englewood Cliffs, N.J. 1964, pp. 447, 451.

10. Op. cit., p. 190.

11. Stark, Rodney and Charles Y. Glock, 'Prejudice and the Churches', Chapter 3 in Charles Y. Glock and Ellen Siegelman, *Prejudice USA*, Praeger, New York 1969, pp. 70–95.

12. Op. cit.

13. Op. cit.

3 Some Aspects of Race and Religion in Britain

Clifford Hill

THE whole subject of race relations with its enormous significance for international relationships is one of great complexity and one which provides a very fruitful and fascinating field for both the sociologist and the social anthropologist. The area of race and religion, however, is one that has been largely ignored by sociologists in this country although not in America. It is a subject whose complexity is added to by the very large number of interacting variables. In order to illustrate some of the complexities involved it will be useful, by a way of introduction, to outline some of the most significant factors.

1. In the first place it is important to recognize that there is no homogeneous immigrant community in Britain. The immigrants do not represent a society in any valid sociological sense. This can be demonstrated quite simply by a look at the national origins of the various New Commonwealth immigrant population groups in this country. The 1966 Sample Census revealed that there were just over a quarter of a million immigrants from the Caribbean, just under a quarter of a million from India, 73,000 from Pakistan, 59,000 from Cyprus, 89,000 from Africa and 66,000 others. This docs not include the 155,000 who were born in the Old Commonwealth, that is in Australia, New Zealand and Canada. Neither do these figures include the children born to Commonwealth immigrants in Britain.

Even if we merely take the immigrants from the five major groups without attempting to break down the 'others' it is clear that the immigrants from the New Commonwealth are diversified in terms of national and ethnic origins, language, custom, religion and education to mention but a few. Thus to speak of the immigrants as a 'society' or to undertake any form of sociological enquiry, without taking account of the socio-cultural diversities amongst them, is quite meaningless.

2. Although the immigrants and their children are estimated to number about 1·2 million in a population of 54·6 million, thus representing roughly 2% of the total population of England and Wales, their pattern of settlement has not been even. The 1961 Census figures revealed that two-thirds of all the Commonwealth immigrants in Britain were living in six large urban areas. Of these two-thirds lived in London. Figures from the 1966 Sample Census show that in Greater London there were 310,190 in a total population of 7·7 million, thus representing 4·03% of the London population. In the West Midland conurbation there were 82,000 Commonwealth immigrants in a total population of 2·37 million, thus representing 3·46% of the West Midland population.

The bulk of the immigrants have therefore settled in a limited number of highly industrialized urban areas, densely populated and characterized by some of the most complex social problems of the era. These problems existed long before the coloured immigrants began to arrive in the early 1950s. Indeed, some of them have been problem areas ever since the Industrial Revolution! Shortages of housing, education and the provision of the basic social services have intensified and complicated the problems of the developing multi-racial communities. For the immigrants, there were all the problems associated with the change from rural to urban settings, and from agrarian to industrial pursuits, intensified by cultural barriers, ethnic prejudices and the backwash of social problems already existing in the settlement areas.

3. The third factor to be noted is the presence in Britain of deeply entrenched prejudiced attitudes which have formed a hostile environment for the settlement of coloured immigrants in this country. It is well known that mild xenophobia is characteristic of British attitudes towards most foreigners and indeed towards most strangers. This is not the place, neither is there any great need, to demonstrate the validity of the statement that there exists a considerable amount of colour prejudice in Britain. The 1967 PEP Report brought this to the public attention with complacency-shattering clarity.[1]

4. A fourth factor to be noted concerns the social demography of the church in Britain. This is a relevant factor because in spite of the presence of large numbers of Sikhs and Muslims, it is still true that well over half the total number of immigrants from the New Commonwealth have come from Christian origins. Moreover, due to the universalistic message of Christianity and its widespread missionary

endeavours over the past 200 years, there are few of the immigrants who have not come into contact with some form of Christian institution before coming to Britain. Hence it is necessary to note the dynamic situation of institutionalized Christianity in Britain and in particular it is relevant to note both the effects of secularization in an increasingly technological society and the significance of class and status variables.

The modern church is a disproportionately middle-class institution, thriving mainly in certain favoured middle-class residential areas, and languishing in the depressed urban working-class areas. It is in these latter areas, where the churches are weakest, that the immigrants have settled. The lack of lay leadership and financial resources in many urban churches makes them unattractive to the clergy and this often results in the least able, rather than the most able, men going there. This, of course, is a generalization that is patently untrue in certain notable instances where gifted individuals are exercising courageous and remarkable ministries, but it is all too pathetically true in a very large number of other cases.

Thus churches which have been least able to make an impact on the local population and to exercise an effective ministry in areas of complex social problems, have been called upon to face the further complicating issue of immigration. Many of the areas of high-density immigrant settlement contain churches whose congregations are reduced to a mere handful of elderly worshippers meeting in ageing, decaying, outdated buildings and ministered to by disillusioned or elderly ministers. It is small wonder that these tiny Christian communities have been bewildered by their rapidly changing social surroundings and have been unable to provide any effective ministry to immigrants.

The welcome accorded to immigrants in English churches has in some instances been embarrassingly warm. This has often been interpreted by the immigrant as another example of white patronage. At the polar extreme the commonest charge made by Christian immigrants, particularly West Indians, is that they have *not* been made welcome in English churches. Many churchgoers in the twilight zones represent the last remaining vestiges of middle-class 'respectability' in their areas. They remember with nostalgic sentiment the days when their churches were full and when institutional Christianity had great social significance in the neighbourhood. They also note with strong disapproval the greatly changed social and moral values in the community. These changes in values, together with the numerical weakness of the church, they associate with the changes in the structure and composition of the population. Coloured immigrants who are visible newcomers are thus seen as symbols of all these changes and as such are an out-group clearly exposed to hostility.

What I am suggesting is that there is some evidence for the belief that there may be higher levels of negative ethnic attitudes to be found among church members in certain areas and under certain conditions than the average for the indigenous population either nationally or in the particular locality. My own investigations indicate that there is a correlation between high scores of ethnocentricity and the threat, either real or imagined, to the continued existence of a particular local church. This is a field in which there is a need for investigations on a much wider scale before any firm conclusions can be drawn.

5. The fifth factor to note is that in spite of the weakness of the churches in the areas of immigrant settlement there have been, and are at present, some fine creative pieces of work being carried out by Christians both through the churches and other social-work agencies. There is the Methodist Notting Hill project; there is the Anglican Inter-Racial Club in Clapham; there is the Friends' Neighbourhood House in Islington, to quote just three London examples of imaginative pieces of work. Many other examples could be given of similar activities in Bradford, Birmingham, Sheffield, Leeds, Manchester, Wolverhampton and a host of other towns and cities. In many cases this work is not merely on the level of religious activities, neither is it concerned only with Christians, but with bridging the gap between immigrants of non-Christian faiths and the host population by extending the hand of friendship.

It is unfortunately true that the value of many of these creative pieces of work is being lost or diminished for lack of locally-based action research whereby some evaluation or comparative assessment could take place. If this were done the results could be of great pragmatic value for those in similar situations in other areas.

6. The sixth point to make is that such research as has been done has served largely to underline the need for further research. Among studies of Asians in Britain, Eric Butterworth's *A Muslim Community in Britain*[2] is particularly interesting. Butterworth based his enquiry upon Bradford and found that the gap between the immigrants and the Christian churches was very wide. In 1,000 Pakistani

households he only found one Christian family and they were members not of a church of one of the major denominations but of a small Christian sect. Butterworth's survey was very limited and he does not attempt an analysis of the reasons for the gap between the Christians and Muslims in Bradford.

There is no equivalent study of Sikhs in Britain, although there is some research in progress. Desai's *Indian Immigrants in Britain*[3] has some useful points on religion; so too does William Israel's review of immigrants in Slough under the title *Colour and Community*.[4] Then there are some very useful background essays in a symposium edited by Robin Oakley entitled *New Backgrounds: The Immigrant Child at Home and at School*.[5] There are so far no published studies of African religious groups in Britain, but some research is in progress.

On the West Indian side there is nothing more up to date than my own *West Indian Migrants and the London Churches*, published in 1963.[6] About the same vintage also is *God's People*,[7] Malcolm Calley's survey of the sectarian patterns of West Indians in Britain. There is evidence that the situation has changed a good deal since then, particularly in regard to the development of immigrant sect organizations to which further reference will be made.

The need for more research into the religious aspects of race relations in Britain is underlined by the manifest importance of religion in the lives of the great majority of the immigrants. For most of them religion is inseparable from the socio-cultural aspects of behaviour, hence the significance of religion for the social scientist and hence also the pragmatic value of research in this field in terms of promoting a greater understanding of the immigrants. I believe that knowledge of the religious beliefs and practices of immigrants would be of considerable value in dispelling the clouds of ignorance, the fears and fantasies and the unfavourable stereotypes of the indigenous British towards their new coloured neighbours.

7. This brings me to my seventh point, which concerns culture change and conflict. One hardly needs to set up elaborate research to demonstrate the hypothesis that culture differences have a high degree of significance in the production of hostile inter-ethnic attitudes. There is a great wealth of folk-lore on this subject. There is, moreover, no shortage of impressionistic material in the speeches of politicians, in the writings of journalists and in reports on the mass media. Why we *do* need more research, and I make no apology for repeating

this, is to enlighten the whole subject of culture change and conflict. Let me give three examples of what I mean.

Local English people are often shocked by differences in behaviour patterns that they observe between immigrants and themselves. They notice for example, that West Indians have different attitudes towards marriage and consequently different sex mores. The absence of any attempt to hide what are considered deviant sex patterns has often been an affront to local white people. I know an English clergyman who recalls how he was taken aback when he first began work in an immigrant settlement area. A young West Indian couple went to him to arrange a wedding. After he had taken note of all the details, and they had fixed the date and so on, they showed no inclination to go but clearly had something else on their minds. Then at last the girl said, 'And whilst we're here, parson, we'd like to book the christening.' He made some remark to the effect that this was rather anticipating a happy event. They looked puzzled for a moment and then the girl said, 'Well, we'd like to get the date booked because he's already three months old.'

It is impossible to understand the West Indian attitudes towards sex and marriage without looking at the whole subject in the context of their social history and the development of a Caribbean culture out of the matrix of plantation slavery. Under British colonial laws, for much of the period of slavery, marriage was illegal for slaves. Children were brought up in the care of the old women of the estate who were too old for work in the field gangs. Thus developed the matriarchal system basic to present-day West Indian society.

The slaves saw marriages take place with great pomp and ceremony and religious sanctity in white society and amongst the fair coloured. After the church service there was music and dancing at the Great House right through the night, and all the relatives and friends of the bride and groom for many miles around came to join in the festivities. This still represents the ideal type of marriage for the West Indian peasant classes. Marriage is strongly identified with economic and status factors. Hence they do not normally marry until they can afford to entertain the whole of their kinship group and friends and neighbours for miles around. Thus 'Common-law Marriage', or faithful concubinage, is the normal pattern of family relationships among the West Indian working classes, and marriage does not normally take place until the required level of economic security has been achieved.

Local English people who have little or no knowledge of the West Indian background see the sex practices of these immigrants as deviant and potentially morally corrupting. They add to the stereotype of the sexual potency of the Negro and stir up fears in the minds of parents of teenage girls against even the most ingenuous forms of inter-racial contact at, for example, the youth club level.

An example of the way in which similar fears are operating in the opposite direction may be seen in the attitudes of Pakistanis in two respects. They look upon English girls as being indecently clad, having wrong attitudes towards sex and marriage and as being potentially morally corrupting for their own children. They see contact with young English people as representing a threat that may undermine the whole basic structure of the family and their traditional cultural patterns, including the subordination of women.

This culture is rooted in religious belief and in this respect they see Christian education in schools as presenting a threat to their own culture and to their authority over their children. In reaction to this threat, as both Butterworth and Goodall in *New Backgrounds*[8] have pointed out, many Pakistani parents, no doubt under pressure from the local Imam, are sending their children to the Mosque for intensive religious instruction. Goodall found that the majority of Pakistani children in Bradford are receiving instruction at the mosque for between fifteen and twenty hours each week, learning Arabic and Urdu and reading the Koran and learning the Namaz (the forms of prayer and codes of behaviour of the Islamic faith).

I do not wish to give the impression that all immigrant parents are reacting to the situation in Britain in a highly conservative manner. There is evidence for a considerable degree of cultural change taking place among even the most strongly traditional groups. For example, as long ago as 1964 in William Israel's survey of Slough[9] he found that 20% of male Sikhs were shaving their beards, cutting their hair and abandoning turbans. Admittedly his sample was small, but the reasons given by his respondents for these major changes were highly significant. These varied from the need for industrial safety to the desire to lessen the social distance between themselves and members of the host society.

The uncut hair, and hence the turban and the comb in the hair, are two of the five 'K's sacred to Sikhs and obligatory for all male Sikhs as part of the outward and visible signs of their membership of their religious society.

All culture change involves conflict either within the individual or in his relationships within his own reference group or with wider society. To this extent the pressures to conformity with host society norms which are acting upon the religio-cultural practices of the immigrants are involving them in conflict. Again this is an area which calls for research and about which we know all too little at the moment.

West Indians and the English churches

To turn now to the religious situation of West Indian immigrants and their belief patterns and practices. First I want to look at the West Indian's relationships with local English churches.

The West Indian comes from a predominantly English cultural background in which most of his major social institutions are based upon English ideal types. Probably the most outstanding example of this is religion, while the most notable exception is the family. All the major branches of the Western church are firmly established in the West Indies, and their patterns of worship as well as their beliefs and practices are very largely identical with those found in similar churches in this country. Thus it would seem reasonable to expect that the churches could provide, if not an open sesame into wider society, at least a reference group with which the incoming migrant could readily identify himself and in which he could find unconditional acceptance. In functional terms, one could expect the indigenous churches to be providing a matrix of integration which in time would lead to full assimilation and to similar acceptance in wider society. Such, however, has not been the case.

The figures I gave in *West Indian Migrants and the London Churches*[10] showed that an average of 69% of the total population in the British Caribbean attend regularly one or other of the six major branches of the Christian church – the Roman Catholic, the Church of England, the Baptist, Congregational, Methodist and Presbyterian churches. A survey of attendance of West Indians at the same churches in the whole of Greater London in comparison with the census figures of West Indians in the Greater London area revealed that only 4% of the immigrants are regular in church attendance.

Clearly some major variables have been injected into the situation to disturb what we should otherwise have expected to be the normal pattern of behaviour. I want to offer four observations relevant to this situation.

1. The first is that the West Indian's change in churchgoing habits must be seen in the context of the total immigrant situation and of the 'culture shock' he experiences on coming to Britain. The great bulk of West Indian immigrants come, not from the towns or from the middle classes or from the professions, but from rural areas and from the peasant strata. Thus the change they experience is a radical one. It is a change from the extended family and kinship system of a simple society to the loneliness of individual living; from a simple rural agrarian economy to a competitive, industrial economy; from a simple village society to a complex urban society fragmented by advanced technology and individuation. Thus the West Indian experiences all the *anomie* of living in a modern, complex, urban, industrial society multiplied a thousandfold by the effects of a sudden and radical culture change. It is small wonder that his religious practices are affected together with all the rest of his previously accepted beliefs and behaviour patterns.

2. Secondly, it cannot be over-emphasized that the West Indian comes from a largely English colonial cultural background with a strong pro-British orientation, and that his expectations of life in Britain and of attitudes towards him have been very largely coloured by this background. Three hundred years of British rule have left their mark. Britain is looked upon as the 'mother country' and thus migration is seen quite simply as 'going home'. The West Indian expects to be accepted in Britain freely, easily and naturally, on terms of absolute equality without distinction of race or colour. Thus when he encounters prejudice he is not merely shocked, he is bitterly disappointed and disillusioned.

I believe that the West Indians' rejection of the church in Britain is not merely or even primarily a rejection of their beliefs or of their traditional religious affiliations, but is a symbol of their disillusionment with, and dissociation from, the society and its culture which has rejected them. The success of immigrant Pentecostal organizations, to which further reference will be made, in attracting many immigrants who were formerly members of one of the major churches or denominations, lends support to the belief that it is *socio-cultural* rather than religious rejection which is taking place among West Indians in Britain.

3. Thirdly, we must return to the point that the English churches

today are largely middle-class institutions enshrining middle-class values. This is certainly no new development in some of them. A correspondent in the *British Weekly* as long ago as November 1892 asked 'What can be done to give working men a place and influence in the Government of our churches?' A Congregationalist gave one answer; 'You must abolish the unwritten law that the first qualification to be a deacon is that a man should possess a cheque book', while a Baptist deacon writing the following week in the same journal denied that anything could be done: 'For official positions in most churches,' he said, 'a higher measure of education is desirable than is usually possessed by working men. Business ability, tact in dealing with men, knowledge of affairs, all come in as requisites.'[11]

E. R. Wickham, in his study of Sheffield,[12] denied that the church has ever commanded the support of the working classes in Britain. But the point we are making here is that the situation in the West Indies is totally different in that the churches *do* command the widespread support of the working classes. Hence when the West Indian comes to Britain and goes to church, for the first time in his life he experiences a sense of social distance between himself and other members of the congregation. He feels shabbily dressed, poorly educated and at grave social disadvantage in comparison with his middle-class, socially secure, white fellow worshippers.

4. The fourth relevant factor is also in terms of class and social distance. It is that the immigrants have settled in the densely populated twilight urban areas of our towns and cities and that the majority of them work in unskilled or semi-skilled occupations. In other words they live and work alongside the English working-class artisans who, as we have already pointed out, are very largely absent from our churches.

Now although the newly-arrived West Indian immigrant tends to reject the British and everything pertaining to them, once he has got over his initial culture shock and period of disillusionment he tends to reorientate himself and readjust his social perspectives. He still has his traditionally strong regard for the 'British way of life' and desire for acceptance into British society. He usually sees this in terms of an acceptance by his neighbours and workmates. He also discovers amongst them a high degree of religious rejection, or at least rejection of institutional forms of Christianity in Britain. Thus he sees that to go to church and to persist in an attempt to gain acceptance there will not help in the achievement of his social goals. In fact it will do the reverse and will merely add further to the social distance between himself and his white workmates and neighbours.

Pentecostalists

Among Christians from the West Indies, the only religious organizations enjoying any numerical success are the sects. These are usually Pentecostal Assemblies such as the various branches of the Church of God or the Seventh Day Adventists. Here again the most striking phenomenon is lack of success of the indigenous Pentecostal Assemblies and Seventh Day Adventist organizations. Almost without exception those who are attracting large numbers of coloured worshippers are organized by immigrant leaders and their congregations and are wholly composed of coloured people.

The rapid growth of immigrant Pentecostal Assemblies may be illustrated by a single example. In 1965 Malcolm Calley (*God's People: West Indian Pentecostal Sects in England*) found that the New Testament Church of God, the largest of the Pentecostal immigrant sects in Britain, had a total of 23 congregations scattered throughout the country, but mainly centred in the London and Birmingham areas. Two years later (in an unpublished survey for the Independent Television Authority as part of an Advisory Report on Immigrant Religious Broadcasting), I found that they had a total of 61 congregations with a total membership of 10,500. They had 15 full-time ministers, a theological college training 20 students for the full-time ministry, a national headquarters in Birmingham, and the whole country was divided into eight provinces, each with a full time 'overseer'. Forty-four were meeting in rented premises and 17 owned their own church buildings. These latter were purchased from one or other of the major denominations in depressed urban working-class areas where the traditional churches could no longer maintain a congregation.

The success of the Pentecostal Assemblies, wholly organized and led by immigrants, underlines the tragic failure of the traditional English churches to hold the allegiance of those immigrants who were already established Christians before coming to England. To see this failure in its true perspective one must bear in mind that in the West Indies, Pentecostalists represent only 5% of the total Christian community. Also my own investigations indicate that a large number of those who are now being attracted to immigrant Pentecostal sects were formerly members of one or other of the six major branches of the Christian church. Again there is scope for considerably more research in this field.

I see three factors which at least in part account for the rapid growth of the West Indian Pentecostal sects in Britain.

1. The first factor concerns the religious orientation of Pentecostalism. In the West Indies most Pentecostal sects preach a doctrine of exclusive membership based upon strict observance of religious and ethical requirements. Sexual laxity is condemned, so are smoking and swearing, the use of cosmetics and any kind of adornment or artificial aids to beauty such as the straightening of the hair. Sect members accept a doctrine of conditional immortality based upon salvation through repentance and regeneration. They look upon themselves as the 'Saints' and all who do not share their beliefs and practices as being outside the realms of salvation and destined for Hell. Thus they are used to regarding themselves as a separatist society, so that social rejection by wider society such as they experience on coming to Britain is no new experience to them. Thus we may expect their faith to have a higher survival rate than that of West Indians brought up in the traditional churches.

2. The leaders of the immigrant sects in Britain, having experienced rejection in wider society, claim also to have experienced the same rejection within English Pentecostal institutions and have thus withdrawn and formed their own sect organization. These are vigorously proselytizing movements. There is also a flavour of nationalism and ethnocentricity about their meetings that must appeal to the expatriate West Indian. Thus the immigrant's sense of alienation from wider society, plus his need for the consolation and support of religion in a situation of stress, provide a strong motivation for him to ally himself with others who share his experience and who have found the consolation they require in a sect organization.

3. The third factor accounting for the recent successes of immigrant Pentecostal organizations I see in terms of deprivation. Glock (in Lee and Marty, *Religion and Social Conflict*[13]) has reminded us that deprivation need not be economic. Certainly the great majority of West Indians in Britain are not suffering from economic deprivation. Economically they are far better off than they were in their home-lands, but they are experiencing both ethnic and status depri-

vation. I have many times heard West Indians say that they had never thought of themselves as being 'coloured' until they came to Britain. Because of his colour the West Indian is forced into a particular status-group that has all the characteristics of immobility common to a caste. Incidentally, deprivation is the most significant factor in the whole field of race relations in Britain today, even in terms of the attitudes of the English working classes in the deprived urban areas to the coming of the coloured people. If we apply Runciman's theory of Relative Deprivation to the British colour situation we can find there a sociological theory to account for the British working-class racialist attitudes such as were seen in the phenomenon of the marches of dockers and meat porters in support of Enoch Powell. Deprivation has the effects of driving together in social solidarity members of the pariah group. Thus the rapid rise in membership of immigrant-organized Pentecostal sects may well be a religious response to the experience of social deprivation.

There are three observations I would like to make in regard to this phenomenon of immigrant Pentecostalism in Britain, which gives every sign of becoming a major religious movement within the next decade or so.

1. In the first place, I believe there is good evidence to support the belief that what we are witnessing is the rise of a new millennial movement. In the sermons I have heard preached by immigrant Pentecostalists in recent years, time after time there has been the emphasis upon social conditions in Britain, the wickedness of wider society, the rejection by that society of the values for which Pentecostalists stand, and the rejection by Pentecostalists of the values of wider society. There is also both a this-worldly and an other-worldly context to the message of salvation, but the this-worldly emphasis is always presented within the context of a sudden divine intervention through the Second Coming of Christ, when those who now suffer under the yoke of oppression will be justified and enjoy the benefits brought by the Messiah.

2. Secondly, it is well known that when religiously orientated millennial movements fail to satisfy by achieving the desired salvation, there is a tendency for the members to seek political outlets for their social goals. Some of these signs can already be seen, as disaffected Pentecostal sect members associate themselves with what can only be described as 'Black Power' groups. The danger with any millennial-type religious movement is that if there is no pro-

gress made in terms of the removal of the conditions of deprivation and the achievement of desired social goals, other and more violent forms of millennialism often follow.

3. Thirdly, I see some danger of the development of a form of 'apartheid religion' in Britain due to the establishment of immigrant religious sects. While it is possible to justify, on grounds of social and psychological need, the meeting of first generation expatriates in exclusive societies, there is grave danger of perpetuating some form of apartheid where the expatriates are ethnically and visibly distinct from wider society.

This danger is being intensified in the present situation by the exclusive religious beliefs of the Pentecostalists and by the fact that they are taking their children to their meetings and instructing them in their doctrines. Thus, the children of immigrants, born in Britain and wholly educated in the British educational system, are being separated from their peer groups for religious purposes. The exclusive nature of the beliefs and practices of sect members must inevitably separate these children from their white friends and neighbours and add further social distance between them as they enter adulthood.

In conclusion I want to offer two very brief observations. The first is concerned with the role of the churches in the contemporary situation of race relations in Britain. The churches' failure to meet the immigrant situation must be seen not simply as a failure in the field of race relations but as one aspect of their failure to understand and to grapple with a whole range of problems in contemporary Britain and in particular in the deprived urban areas. The churches do not need to work out a new policy on race relations. Their paramount need is to devise a new strategy of evangelism and social witness in urban Britain. The presence of coloured immigrants in these areas should not be tackled as a separate issue but as one facet, or a series of aspects, of a total situation. Thus the churches' prime need is for a new understanding of the significance of their own role and presence in urban industrial British society.

Secondly, we need to know a lot more about the whole process of cross-cultural fertilization in the developing multi-racial populations of urban Britain. Many of the tensions and conflicts that are at present to be found, both among the immigrants and members of the host society, stem not merely from their ignorance of the religious beliefs and practices and cultural patterns of each other but from

organizational and structural disorientations in society due to our
failure to understand the nature of the processes involved.

NOTES

1. A somewhat more optimistic view of race relations in Britain was put forward in E. J. B. Rose (ed.), *Colour and Citizenship* (OUP 1969) which did not show the high levels of prejudice in the white population reflected in other studies including the PEP Report. Daniel Lawrence, writing in *New Society* of 21 August 1969, held that the *Colour and Citizenship* report was over-optimistic. He indicated a number of areas in which prejudice was strong.

This controversy among sociologists in Britain as to the exact level of ethnic prejudice will probably continue for a long time to come due to the difficulty of establishing any exact criteria for the measurement of prejudice, or the formulation of a scale which would indicate where the line between prejudice and tolerance should be drawn.

This is not the place to undertake a critique of the methodology of the 'Five Year Survey', but the writer takes the view that there is evidence to indicate that the *Colour and Citizenship* report has underestimated the level of colour prejudice in Britain.

2. E. Butterworth, *A Muslim Community in Britain*, Church of England, Board of Social Responsibility 1968.

3. R. Desai, *Indian Immigrants in Britain*, OUP 1963.

4. W. Israel, *Colour and Community*, Slough Council of Social Service 1964.

5. R. Oakley (ed.), *New Backgrounds*, OUP 1968.

6. C. Hill, *West Indian Migrants and the London Churches*, OUP 1963.

7. M. Calley, *God's People*, OUP 1965.

8. Oakley, op. cit., p.90.

9. Israel, op. cit., p.16.

10. Hill, op. cit., p.22.

11. K. S. Inglis, *Churches and the Working Classes in Victorian England*, Routledge & Kegan Paul 1963, p. 115.

12. E. R. Wickham, *Church and People in an Industrial City*, Lutterworth Press 1957.

13. C. Y. Glock, 'The Role of Deprivation in the Origin and Evolution of Religious Groups', R. Lee and M. Marty (eds.), *Religion and Social Conflict*, OUP 1964.

4 Local and Cosmopolitan Aspects of Religious Activity in a Northern Suburb

David B. Clark

Traditional and non-traditional

After the last war, and in large part due to the immense task of rebuilding bomb-scarred cities and reshaping a society in a state of flux, the British sociological scene witnessed the appearance of a large number of community studies analysing and assessing urban and rural settlements in such places as far apart as Bethnal Green (East London) and Glynceiriog (Denbighshire), Barton Hill (Bristol) and Gosforth (Cumberland).[1] Though many of these studies were full of excellent descriptive material and made extremely interesting reading in their own right, they frequently lacked a clear theoretical framework to facilitate comparison of the settlements investigated. Only in quite recent years has any attempt been made to bring these studies together to form a coherent picture of the nature of British community life.[2]

None the less, out of the wealth of descriptive detail provided by such community studies, certain concepts of general and lasting value did emerge. Two of these were the terms first formulated by Stacey in her study of Banbury: the traditional and the non-traditional.[3] The twin concepts were developed as a result of her study of the tensions arising in the social life of Banbury some years after a large aluminium factory had begun production there. Stacey discovered that the main social divisions within Banbury society were not simply between those of different social class or even between the natives and the newcomers, but between those she called 'the traditionalists' and 'the non-traditionalists'.

Throughout her description of Banbury, Stacey specifies, though never in a very systematic way, a large number of features characteristic of her two types. She finds traditionalism easier to define mainly because it typifies 'a group with considerable local loyalty and, moreover, solidarity . . . , a group bound together by common history and tradition, with a recognized social structure and having certain common values'.[4] Non-traditionalism is a more elusive concept simply because it gives rise to no single or solidary grouping: 'It is typical of non-traditionalism in Banbury that it is not a unity: the only factor which non-traditionalists have in common is non-conformity in some respect to the traditions of Banbury.'[5]

While Stacey was studying the phenomenon of social change in Banbury, other students were discovering similar features elsewhere. In many ways akin to Stacey's traditional type were Brennan's 'local system',[6] Mogey's 'status-assenters',[7] and Elias and Scotson's 'established' residents.[8] Similar to Stacey's non-traditional type were Brennan's 'unoriented working class' and 'anglicized middle class', Mogey's 'status-dissenters', and Elias and Scotson's 'outsiders'. Behind both sets of concepts there lay the ever seminal work of Tönnies on the 'Gemeinschaft' and 'Gesellschaft' types of society.[9]

Stacey had obviously drawn attention to a typology of major importance in community study, although her traditional and non-traditional types were analytic concepts and were never used to build any particular theory of social change. Yet the actual *terms* used to describe her two types of resident (traditional and non-traditional) remain ambiguous. As Stacey herself realized, certain features of traditional community life in Banbury were found in other contexts, such as by Brennan in South-west Wales, to be characteristic of a non-traditional life-style.[10] The terms traditional and non-traditional prove in fact to be too relative, too closely tied to a particular settlement or a particular period in its development, to be generally applied with any precision. It is thus necessary to look for more sociologically useful terms to sum up the outstanding features of the typology discussed above.

Local and cosmopolitan

There is no doubt that of all those characteristics distinguishing Stacey's traditional and non-traditional types, and those of the other writers mentioned, one appears as of overriding importance; whether residents in any settlement are locally oriented in attitude and behaviour, or whether their outlook and activities are very much more shaped by the wider world beyond. In giving typological form to the phenomena described by Stacey and others, it is thus more precise to employ terms specifically referring to the local or non-local orientation of the life-style of residents. In what follows the terms coined by Merton, in his study of the American town of 'Rovere', will be used.[11] Describing the sort of phenomena to which Stacey gives the name traditional, Merton uses the term 'local', and in describing a way of life similar to that pursued by Stacey's non-traditional resident, Merton uses the term 'cosmopolitan'.

Mobility: spatial, social and cognitive

It is, however, of value to go one step beyond the typology used by Stacey and by Merton and ask what it is that determines whether a person becomes a local or a cosmopolitan. In answer to this question students of community point to one dominating factor in moulding the activity and social relationships of residents: mobility. Perraton writes: 'Although it is possible that certain aspects of the new physical environment (such as better houses and a more open layout) may have helped to confirm new social patterns, it seems probable that the most important factor in any social change has been the move away from daily contact with kinsfolk, and the old social environment with its familiar patterns of behaviour.'[12]

Mobility has three distinguishable facets, all very closely related and all having an important influence on whether residents of a particular settlement are locals or cosmopolitans. First, there is *spatial mobility*; the extent to which people have above all moved their place of residence, but also referring to the degree of regular movement they are involved in to and from school, work, and main shopping and recreational centres. Secondly, there is *social mobility*; the extent to which people have climbed the social scale over the years. Thirdly, there is what is called here *cognitive mobility*. This term describes the degree to which people are open to and assimilate ideas, values and experiences which come to them from beyond their own immediate environment. Cognitive mobility is characterized by the readiness to appreciate other people's point of view and by the ability to be critical of the life-style of one's own social circle.

The Case-study: Oakcroft

This introduction has been necessary to prepare the way for the

subsequent application of the concepts mentioned (local and cosmopolitan; spatial, social and cognitive mobility), to the life of the
church in a northern suburb. For just as the local–cosmopolitan
division, with its consequent tensions, permeates societies such as
those found in Banbury and 'Rovere', so too does it deeply affect
the church as an institution within society.

The specific focus of attention is the religious life of residents of
a working-class suburb on the edge of a northern industrial city.
This suburb is here given the name of 'Oakcroft'. In the mid-1960s
Oakcroft was a distinct settlement with a narrow belt of fields, woods
and old colliery workings and spoil heaps separating it on all sides
from neighbouring suburbs. It was somewhat off the beaten track
with main roads to nearby towns by-passing it at some distance.

Oakcroft had originally been a farming settlement, but from the
mid-nineteenth century the local collieries had dominated the
physical and social scene. The population mushroomed after the
collieries had opened and by 1901 there were 7,830 residents. Until
1921 Oakcroft remained an important part of an urban district
independent of the nearby city, and its residents enjoyed their
relative isolation and self-sufficiency. However, the first half of this
century saw Oakcroft lose a good deal of its previous vitality. Its
population increased very little, many of its middle class moved to
more salubrious parts of the city, it lost its economic and administrative independence and it rapidly became 'just another suburb'. After
the Second World War three council house estates were built in
Oakcroft, the largest one going up in the early 1960s. By 1966 the
population had risen to 9,655, with the post-war estates containing
42% of the adult residents. Though a small amount of private
development had taken place, by the mid-1960s the residents of
Oakcroft fell into two main groups: the old residents and their
families who had been born and/or bred in Oakcroft inhabiting the
old village, and the newcomers inhabiting the post-war estates.

In 1966 the following religious bodies were active, in order of
appearance on the Oakcroft scene: the Society of Friends, the
Methodists (two churches), the Congregationalists, the Church of
England, the Salvation Army and the Assemblies of God (Pentecostalists). The following analysis will be confined to the Methodist
churches, undoubtedly the two strongest congregations in Oakcroft,
though what is written of these remains typical of *all* the other
religious bodies in the area.

Of the two Methodist church buildings, the oldest was Wesley (ex-Wesleyan), erected in 1878, though a small Wesleyan chapel had been in existence in Oakcroft as long ago as 1814. Some 300 yards down the street and on the opposite side stood Bethel (ex-United Methodist Free Church), built in 1889, though the original society had broken away from the Wesleyans in 1850. Between these two buildings lay a third Methodist church (ex-Primitive) originally built in 1905 but closed in 1951 and since 1966 used as a child welfare clinic.

Locals and cosmopolitans in Oakcroft Methodism

1. *Participants*

In 1966 the membership of Wesley Methodist church stood at 133 and of Bethel Methodist church at 112. There was very little 'dead wood' (i.e. those who were physically able yet rarely attended worship) on the membership rolls though Sunday congregations were smaller than the official membership figures. At Wesley the average attendance on a normal Sunday morning was about 25 and in the evening about 60; at Bethel the figures were respectively 20 and 75. At Bethel particularly most of those attending the morning service were 'twicers'.

The sex ratio within the two Methodist churches was heavily biased, especially amongst the 45 and over age-group, in favour of the women who made up 65% of the total membership at Wesley and 60% at Bethel. These figures compare with a sex ratio in the Oakcroft population as a whole of 52% women to 48% men.[13]

The age of the members of the two Methodist churches is shown in the following table.

AGE OF METHODIST MEMBERS

Age group	Wesley	Bethel	Oakcroft as a whole
15–19	11	21	11
20–29	5	7	19
30–44	15	15	30
45–59	35	22	23
60+	33	34	17

All figures expressed as percentages to the nearest whole number

It will be noted that Bethel, and to a lesser extent Wesley, had a fairly strong teenage group, that both churches were poorly represented in the 20–44 age group, and that both were well in excess of the surrounding population in the 60+ age group.

The sex and age profile of the two Methodist churches gives a fairly local type picture, i.e. in both congregations the middle aged and especially the elderly, notably elderly women, were dominant. However, those normally possessing a more cosmopolitan outlook were in evidence. Such were the teenage group at both churches. Such also were those younger residents of Oakcroft who, though not officially members, yet had close links with the Methodist churches. For example, Wesley ran a Young Wives' Group with a regular attendance of about 30 (very few of whom were actual church members), and the parents of Sunday School children were evident on quite a few occasions such as Sunday School concerts and Family Services. Of particular note was a group of young couples, all non-churchgoers, who yet met regularly in a house group on the most recently built estate under the leadership of the Methodist minister.

2. *Spatial mobility*

(a) *Locals* The proportion of Methodist church members born and bred in Oakcroft was surprisingly high, 93% at Wesley and 75% at Bethel. As a consequence of residential immobility kinship ties between members were very strong. At Wesley the lay leadership was dominated by the large Smith family, of which four brothers and two sisters, not to mention their partners by marriage, children and in-laws, were extremely prominent in church affairs. At certain church functions, even when non-members were present in considerable numbers, the older members of the Smith family were publicly referred to as 'Uncle Jack', 'Auntie Jane', etc. The Leaders' and Trustees' Meetings at Wesley were in many ways domestic affairs and disagreement was much feared as this meant 'a split in the family' and recriminations outside. The Smiths were related to three or four other fairly large families of some influence at Wesley, and the majority of the church members were linked by some blood tie or marriage relationship. At Bethel kinship links throughout the whole membership were not as close as at Wesley, though church affairs were dominated by two interrelated families, the Browns and the

Wrights. Members of these two families usually formed a majority on the Bethel Leaders' Meeting.

Very few Oakcroft Methodists who moved away seriously thought of joining up with another church, and then only if it were quite impossible 'to get back home'. In all 14 % of the members at Wesley and 12 % of those at Bethel lived outside the area and travelled back regularly on Sundays to visit family and friends and to attend 'their church'. Even when after marriage the children of old residents moved a long way away, they still triumphantly brought their babies back to be christened in the presence of admiring relatives.

The residential immobility of most Methodist members led to the acceptance of the kinship channel as the normative means of recruitment, and both churches looked to the sons and daughters of members to follow in their parents' footsteps. Unfortunately by the mid 1960s even this usually reliable method of maintaining the cause was showing signs of collapse. Families were smaller than in the earlier decades of the century and, as the congregations aged, the supply was steadily running out. Those young people who did become members were normally off in their late teens or early twenties to study, to work or to live elsewhere. This situation resulted in a serious dearth of members in the 20–44 age group at both churches.

Lack of residential mobility led to the emergence of one other feature typical of a locally oriented church life: great pride in and affection for the church building itself. 'We should all treat our church as being as precious as our home', remarked one of the prominent members of Bethel at a Leaders' Meeting. At Wesley the caretaker (a member of the ubiquitous Smith family and a retired builder) spent many long hours in painstaking renovation and maintenance of the premises. He produced a host of potted plants to decorate window ledges and tables, at times scarcely allowing room for chairman and secretary to spread out their papers. Likewise at Bethel the caretaker had lavished countless hours on sweeping, scrubbing and polishing, and every winter morning had risen at 5 a.m. to stoke the boilers. Only when he retired in 1964 did it occur to the Trustees that oil-firing was really preferable. In the mid-1960s both churches, though certainly not wealthy and having some difficulty in finding the amount required by the Circuit, spent several hundred pounds on renovating and redecorating their premises and the plans and colour schemes were discussed with undisguised enthusiasm. There was rarely any shortage of those ready to offer their skills to keep the buildings in good order. Many of the members had after all been baptized and married in and hoped to be buried from a church that was very much 'theirs'.

A majority of the two congregations was not only residentially but occupationally and recreationally immobile too. Here again sex and age played an important part. In Oakcroft many married women who had been born or bred in the area still thought it wrong to go out to work; their place was in the home 'doing for the man and children'. A notable proportion of the male members still worked nearby in the traditional Oakcroft industry, coal mining and its associated branches, with a structure in many ways locally oriented, and much of their leisure time was spent in Oakcroft, often on church premises. Those of both sexes over 60 travelled into the city infrequently, and though outings to the country and the seaside were commonplace in the summer months these were always in the company of other Oakcroft residents.

(b) *Cosmopolitans* If the members of the two Methodist churches were in general spatially immobile, not so the Methodist minister (since 1932 one man had served both the Oakcroft churches). Every three, four or five years (Oakcroft had never kept a minister more than five years except during the last war), he somewhat thankfully departed from the scene. To the locals, the minister was a transient pastor, preacher and co-ordinator (in that order of importance) and, especially at Bethel with its old United Methodist Free Church tradition, was regarded very much as a bird of passage and thus in the last resort dispensable. In 1968 the *new* notice board outside Bethel, in typically local fashion, had the words 'Resident Minister' and his address at the bottom, but his actual name was omitted. Though the local members would lavish a great deal of love and labour on their own churches few felt any responsibility for or took any interest in the condition of the minister's manse (a Circuit and thus implicitly a Society responsibility).

The minister in Oakcroft was regularly faced with the problem of distinguishing his role in a situation where the lay leadership, especially the Smiths at Wesley and the Browns and Wrights at Bethel, was so well established as at times to make him feel expendable. Virtually every new minister since at least the last war had, as a rule early in his ministry in Oakcroft, been involved in a head-on clash with certain of the leading lay figures at either church. His survival and future effectiveness depended on how well he rode this almost inevitable crisis.

Of the residents who had moved into Oakcroft after the last war only a handful became members at Wesley (5% of the membership) or at Bethel (16% of the membership). In 1966, two years after the largest council house estate in Oakcroft had been completed, only four new residents out of its total adult population of 1,226 had taken up Methodist membership. (For a further comment on this situation see below under 'Non-participants'.)

The more cosmopolitan participants in Methodist activities (many of whom were not full members but 'adherents' or attended particular meetings such as the Young Wives' Group) had much less reverence for the church building than the locals. Great was the indignation of the local caretaker and a number of the Trustees at Wesley when the Young Wives failed to clean up adequately after a beauty demonstration. For the cosmopolitans the premises were first and foremost of functional importance and it was they who were usually quickest to complain about splinters from the floors, wooden benches which plucked their stockings, and poor kitchen facilities.

On the whole the young people and adults who daily travelled into the city to school or work were the more cosmopolitan of the Oakcroft Methodists. Constant meeting and mixing with those who did not regard Oakcroft as 'God's own country' gave them a wider perspective on and more critical attitude towards the style of Oakcroft church life (see below under 'Cognitive mobility').

3. *Social mobility*

(a) *Locals* The majority of the members belonging to the two Methodist churches in Oakcroft had been socially immobile (for example, with regard to educational attainment and occupational promotion) throughout their lives. Most of the women had been nothing but housewives and many of the men had remained in the category of unskilled or skilled manual worker.

It was thus common to find ascribed status, typical of a local orientation, of major note in church life. Age was an important factor here. For example, children, however lacking in genuine talent, were greatly praised for public appearances on such occasions as the Sunday School anniversary or church concerts. Their success in the annual Scripture Examination, though invariably all passed, was still regarded by the local adults as extremely meritorious. At Wesley the outstanding honour for a young girl was to be chosen as Sunday School Queen. She was elected according to the votes of her class, though the daughters of prominent Wesley families somehow seemed to manage to head the poll in their year. She was publicly crowned during the Sunday School anniversary, and thereafter spent her year in office on special efforts to raise funds for the church. Photographs of all the Sunday School Queens since the last war hung in the Wesley schoolroom. Ascribed status was related not only to age but also to acquaintance and if a child or adult were particularly well-known to the congregation, applause or congratulations were especially heartfelt (one was, of course, not just applauding or congratulating the person concerned but the family as well).

Achieved status was also typically local in nature for most Oakcroft Methodists. Office in the church, however minor the role, was usually prized by the locals, on one occasion the Methodist minister having to use considerable tact to calm a woman member who had been in charge of the flower rota at Wesley for some years and who had unthinkingly not been reappointed by the Leaders' Meeting. Office in the church brought increased status according to the length it was held. Retirement after long service was frequently acknowledged by some form of public presentation (though an attempt to persuade the 86-year-old choirmistress at Wesley to retire by giving her a presentation for 50 years' service unfortunately failed).

Social immobility still engendered a slight feeling of class consciousness within the two Methodist congregations. In the past Wesley had undoubtedly been the socially superior church and for the locals this belief (though now having little empirical basis) remained. 'I wouldn't think it right to call her by her Christian name', remarked one Bethel lady, the daughter of a miner, of a Wesley woman whose parents had owned property in Oakcroft and who had been friendly with her for many years.

(b) *Cosmopolitans* Both Methodist congregations possessed participants who had moved up the social scale. There were a number of teachers in both churches and men who had advanced to the staff side of industry, not to mention those young people going on to Advanced Level examinations or higher education. Quite a few of the young wives, before raising a family, had been well educated and had held jobs as teachers, nurses and secretaries in the city. Such members and adherents, generally cosmopolitan in outlook, placed the emphasis far more on achieved (as opposed to ascribed) status, and an achieved status not just related to Oakcroft but to the wider world beyond. They might applaud the faltering efforts of the young or the mediocre performance of well-known local friends with the rest, but afterwards they would quietly smile and comment, 'Wasn't that grim!' Yet their attitude to the locals was one of tolerance rather than cynicism; after all it was their way and their church. They were much harder on the visiting preacher who annoyed or bored them; here criticism, especially from the young, was much more outspoken.

Church office was not particularly attractive to the cosmopolitan members; that was more properly the province of the locals. As the latter aged it was thus becoming increasingly difficult to fill even relatively important positions. Appeals for volunteers as well as the growing proportion of local women taking up office in the church only undermined the status-attraction of such posts further.

The most thoroughgoing cosmopolitans amongst the socially mobile members were those young people, some two or three each year at either church, going away to college or university. A number of these broke all links with the church after a year or two and, when visiting home, appeared at church functions merely as a gesture of goodwill to local parents and friends. To such as these young people the whole style of local church life was so traditional as to be suffocating and even rather ridiculous. One notable example here was an intelligent girl belonging to the prominent Wright family at Bethel. She was brought up to attend church regularly, readily became a member and right through her teens played a very active part in the church. A year or so after going to college in the south she stopped attending any place of worship and eventually married a non-Christian boy in a London registry office, her parents being quite unable to comprehend the change to a cosmopolitan life-style.

4. *Cognitive mobility*

(a) *Locals* The majority of members at the two Methodist churches in Oakcroft were cognitively immobile (i.e. their experiences, attitudes and values were very much a product of the local environment). In church life, this meant that the locals were thoroughly at ease with fellow members and adherents whom they had known for many

c

years, but uncertain about and at times suspicious of 'incomers', especially the new residents living on the post-war estates. Thus at Wesley wholehearted approval was given to the launching of a morning club for retired Oakcroft men (though very few were churchgoers they were well known to the Wesley members), whereas much doubt and suspicion were evident when the idea of starting the Young Wives' Group was mooted (for here unfamiliar faces were sure to appear). In 1964 the Oakcroft Council of Churches organized the visitation of the latest council estate as people moved in but, though Methodist members were urged again and again by their minister to share in the work, only a handful participated, the fear of having to make conversation with unknown residents being one very obvious reason for the lack of response.

The close-knit family atmosphere of Oakcroft church life, already referred to more than once, and so precious to the locals, was further enhanced by the very domestic nature of the two church magazines. Great pains were taken by the editors to cover personal details concerning members and adherents and every sickness, success, anniversary or bereavement had to be mentioned. More than once apologies were made in the next issue for omitting some item relating to the fortunes of members which family or friends thought ought to have appeared.

The locals were very much tied to a set routine in ordering church affairs. The pattern of Sunday worship and Sunday School had not changed for decades and attempts by the Methodist minister in the mid-1960s to introduce a few minor changes were not received with outstanding warmth. The totally predictable round of 'special' Sundays (Choir Anniversary, Sunday School Anniversary, Harvest Festival, Church Anniversary, Men's Weekend and so forth) was repeated year after year. Despite poor attendances at the Sunday School anniversary, the Leaders' Meetings at both churches just could not bring themselves to reduce the celebration from two weekends to one. The Bethel Leaders' Meeting in particular spent a great deal of its time racking its brains to suggest the names of chairmen, presidents, preachers, speakers, soloists, etc., to appear at the numerous special events.

The cognitively local orientation of many Methodists was further demonstrated in their attachment to the tangible and practical aspects of church life. At Wesley, for example, the outstanding event of the year was not any of the Christian festivals but the Christmas Market, for which old members who had moved away often made a special effort to return. Raising money and collecting goods to be sold on the great day went on throughout the entire year. It was a particular honour to be asked to take the chair at or open the Market. The day itself was a fever of activity with excitement mounting as the prominently displayed model 'thermometer' indicated the financial total reached. Each stall set out to beat the previous year's figure and there was great satisfaction if it succeeded. Bethel did not have an annual bazaar (and felt themselves a little superior to Wesley because of this) but when in 1966 they mounted a Spring Fayre the enthusiasm surpassed even the zeal of their fellow Methodists up the road. The minister at that time can recall no other occasion during his five years stay in Oakcroft when so many members and adherents at Bethel were so energetically involved in a church event.

Typical of limited cognitive horizons was the ready response of the local members to 'real people' and 'well-loved tunes'. Sermons freely seasoned with personal illustrations and homely anecdotes were especially popular and 'the good old hymns' brought hearty vocal participation. The women's meetings at Wesley and Bethel, mainly made up of the over-60s, were in this respect particularly local. Hymns came from 'Sankey' and simple choruses were popular. Speakers usually chose homely themes and the mood of the address often verged on the sentimental; one afternoon the speaker recited heart-rending poems (some home-made) on such themes as a drowning mariner singing 'Nearer my God to Thee' and the Aberfan disaster. Locals were used to and preferred a minimum of active participation in services and meetings though they engaged energetically in conversation with each other before and after. Only a few of them would be vocal in meetings demanding public discussion and even then their contributions tended to be stereotyped.

The mores evident in Oakcroft church life were largely derived from the Methodism of the late nineteenth century. Gambling and drink were still the main social evils of the day. At one stage the Wesley Trustees were quite strongly divided on whether or not to permit smoking on church premises, and the minister who innocently invited a Marriage Guidance Councillor to speak to the Youth Club was severely reprimanded by a number at the Leaders' Meeting. In 1966 the leading layman at Bethel, a member of the Brown family, addressed a public meeting as follows: 'I'm not worried so much about Vietnam, Rhodesia, the collapse of NATO or China falling out with Russia. I'm worried about the corruption of our people. Corruption of society, not battles, brought down the Roman, Greek and Spanish Empires.'

The cognitively local orientation of the two Methodist churches was especially noticeable in their relations with each other. By the mid-1960s there was a good deal of joint activity (quarterly united services and women's meetings, joint house groups and fellowship meetings). But the preservation of their own traditional way of life and self-identity as a corporate unit loomed large when in 1964 the Methodist minister launched a vigorous attempt to bring the two congregations into one building. After 18 months of protracted negotiations Bethel rejected the only viable scheme, that of moving to a renovated Wesley (though it is quite likely that Wesley would have rejected a plan to move to Bethel). The dominant voice in all meetings and at the end was that of the older members of the leading families previously mentioned.

The members of Wesley and Bethel rarely attended religious functions outside their own building though there was a degree of mutual support for 'special' events. The Oakcroft Council of Churches, which was regarded by most members as a reasonably good thing, had to be extremely careful not to interrupt or challenge those activities well established in either Methodist church. Students visiting Oakcroft for a mission organized by the Council of Churches were not allowed to go on an old people's outing organized by the churches 'in case it created a precedent'.

Knowledge of and interest in church affairs beyond Oakcroft was very limited. Only 18 Methodist households, out of some 200 or more associated with the two churches, took the *Methodist Recorder*. A few of the more conscientious leaders attended Circuit Quarterly Meetings regularly and a fair turn-out was evident at the annual Circuit Rally, but otherwise the Circuit was only regarded of much importance in one respect, that of finance. As the Oakcroft churches had to pay a quarterly Circuit assessment, which Bethel at least was constantly complaining about, they had willy-nilly to keep in touch with this aspect of Circuit business.

The Anglican–Methodist Conversations provoked some discussion in their early stages, being strongly opposed by the Brown and Wright families at Bethel and by the older members of the Smith family at Wesley. The issues to the fore were always the more pragmatic ones (forms of worship, lay control, drink and gambling, and the possible 'take-over' of Methodism). Confusion over the more theological issues was considerable and was demonstrated when the 1966 Circuit Quarterly Meeting passed the Conversations by a single vote (it reversed its decision in 1969) and then approved an amendment objecting to episcopacy.

(b) *Cosmopolitans* The cosmopolitans amongst the two Methodist congregations thought much less than the locals in terms of 'insiders' and 'outsiders'. They were generally less critical of the residents living on the post-war estates and were more inclined to talk in terms of serving the community than 'getting them to church'. The Methodist minister here often found himself caught between his natural sympathy with the cosmopolitan attitude and his institutional duty to the locals.

Cosmopolitan members and adherents were much less predictable in their attendance at Sunday worship and were quite prepared to miss even 'special' events if these clashed with other activities, such as visiting friends, taking the family out into the country, going to the caravan at the seaside or painting and decorating. Many of them had cars, a possession which numerous locals regarded as the biggest threat to church life since the war.

Many cosmopolitans regarded the effort expended on fund raising as unnecessary and much preferred to give money than buy goods at a bazaar. They had rather more of a conscience about spending funds on the premises and when Wesley installed expensive equipment to help the deaf to hear the service certain of them regarded it as 'extravagant'.

The cosmopolitans preferred sermons with 'content' and found the traditional chorus hymns a bit old fashioned. They were much more ready to participate actively in services and meetings than the locals, notably in the monthly house groups where they were prominent in the discussions. However, certain of the younger members found even the house groups too restrictive; 'They're always quoting Scripture and saying the same old things', remarked one young wife. Cosmopolitans were well in evidence in the two most recent groups started at Wesley, the Young Wives' Group which organized evenings of a very varied (and non-religious) sort and visits to places of interest in the city or farther afield, and the Pilgrim Group (though note the local type name) which, catering especially for the 45–59 age group, had speakers on numerous secular topics, held an annual Christmas dinner in a public house in the country and arranged a weekend holiday away for its members.

The values prevalent amongst the more cosmopolitan Methodists were much more liberal than amongst the locals. There was no apology given for having drink in the house and smoking was the norm. Conversation on such matters as politics and sex was far freer.

The influence of the cosmopolitan members enabled the Methodist minister to engage the two churches in serious conversations about uniting. They were 'all for getting together' and when the decisive vote was taken at Bethel they abstained simply because they were unwilling to hurt and possibly unseat the elderly leadership. As one relative newcomer remarked of the two churches rather sadly afterwards, 'They still want to be little puddles.'

Although the cosmopolitans were quite prominent in supporting the activities sponsored by the Oakcroft Council of Churches, like the locals they showed very little interest in church life outside the area. What went on in the larger denominational world was too complicated and too remote to command their interest. Here it was their many other activities and concerns rather than a locally oriented way of life that crowded out participation in what went on beyond the congregation they had linked up with.

Non-participants

In order to appreciate fully the anachronistic position in which the Oakcroft churches found themselves and to set the religious activity of the area in a wider context, it is necessary to say a final word about the many non-participants living round about.

The above analysis of the members and adherents associated with Oakcroft's two Methodist churches inevitably ignores the attitude of the non-churchgoers in the vicinity and whether the latter were themselves locals or cosmopolitans. In 1966 some 3% of Oakcroft's residents attended worship each Sunday at one of the local churches (another 3% attending the Roman Catholic church in a nearby suburb). (It is perhaps interesting to note that in 1912 the number of Oakcroft adults attending worship in the area each Sunday was well over 20%.) In the mid-1960s, therefore, there was a very large number of non-participating residents.

These were divided into the two major groupings mentioned

earlier when introducing the case-study. There were the older residents, born and bred in Oakcroft, who were very much locally
oriented. Though they rarely attended church functions they had
numerous links with the churches either because relatives or friends
of many years' standing still went or because they themselves, in the
hey-day of the Sunday Schools in Oakcroft when about half the
children in the area attended regularly, had participated as youngsters
in religious activities. It was from this group that the Oakcroft
churches in the mid-1960s found recruits for their thriving old
people's clubs.

Secondly, there were the non-participant newcomers who had
moved in mainly since 1955. They consisted predominantly of young
families who were products of the post-war world. Though they
were perhaps not quite as socially or cognitively mobile as certain
residents in the more middle-class suburbs of the city, in comparison
with the Oakcroft locals, especially those attending Oakcroft churches,
they were thoroughly cosmopolitan. Amongst them there were a
very large majority who felt the local churches to be irrelevant and
made no attempt even to send their children to Sunday School.
Though apathy was far more prevalent than antagonism they all
felt the local churches to be more or less superfluous and just 'for
those that like that sort of thing'.

On the other hand there was amongst the newcomers a very small
but very cosmopolitan group, made up of those who had had passing
contact with churches in other parts of the city mainly when young,
who found no attraction in the dominantly local brand of Oakcroft
Methodism and church life in general. It was from amongst this
group of mostly young couples that visitation organized by the
Oakcroft Council of churches and the efforts of the Methodist
minister had produced the non-churchgoing house group mentioned
earlier. It consisted of some two dozen residents, of whom about a
dozen or fifteen met monthly in each other's homes to discuss
religious and secular subjects at some depth. Their cosmopolitan
interests and life-style were so foreign to the local way of life pursued
by the Oakcroft Methodists and other churchgoers that, though
these residents at times showed a deep concern with religious and
social questions, it remained quite impossible to link them successfully
to the existing religious organizations. They continued as an active
and articulate 'religious' group outside the official bodies.

Observations and implications

The division of Oakcroft Methodists into locals and cosmopolitans inevitably suffers the fate of all typologies. One is always dealing with characteristics rather than total persons or groups. Thus there were Oakcroft Methodists who were spatially mobile yet had remained socially and cognitively immobile. There were here and there amongst Methodists born and bred in Oakcroft and who had not ascended the social scale those who were cognitively cosmopolitan. Nevertheless, accepting these qualifications, it would be quite accurate to conclude that the activities and structure of the two Oakcroft Methodist churches were predominantly local in orientation. Where thoroughgoing cosmopolitan members (i.e. those mobile on all counts) were in evidence they tended to let the locals 'have their way' as it was really 'their church', or they confined their activities to one or two more specifically cosmopolitan organizations (such as the Young Wives' Group). In any case many of the younger ones were planning to move away for educational or other reasons. Surrounding the very small number of Oakcroft residents who attended church lay the steadily dwindling body of old, non-church-going and locally oriented natives, and the gradually increasing number of apathetic cosmopolitan newcomers.

In all that has been written above there is no intention of ascribing greater 'value' to either the local or cosmopolitan way of church life. Though one is tempted with Klein to speak of 'cognitive poverty'[14] amongst locals, there are obvious organizational and social strengths and weaknesses in both types of group. For example, the locals might be somewhat narrow in outlook and rigid in behaviour but they were deeply committed to their church and fellow members. The cosmopolitans might be more articulate and wider in understanding and sympathies but they could be erratic in support and unwilling to involve themselves in any regular tasks or service. It is thus misguided, at least sociologically, to attempt to decide which type of church life is 'better'.

On the other hand, it is more than necessary and urgent to pose the major question raised by this case-study as to what form of church life is culturally and organizationally viable in the society in which we now live. The Oakcroft investigation points towards a fundamental dilemma facing many churches today. They appear to be standing as local 'islands' surrounded by an ever encroaching and eroding cosmopolitan 'sea'. Or to be more specific, in Oakcroft the two Methodist churches (as Methodist churches go, still relatively strong and active and certain to continue their dominantly local form of life well into the 1970s) reflect the pattern of society as it existed before 1939, and often before 1914, whilst around live an increasing number of younger residents with a predominantly post-war life-style.

It is true that Oakcroft might not be typical. But the author's fairly wide knowledge of Methodism at least gives him no hesitation in stating that the Oakcroft variety still resembles the form of church life dominant in a notable majority of Methodist societies. In fact, many Methodist churches in inner city and in rural areas still appear to be even more locally oriented than in Oakcroft.

At the present time Methodism, and undoubtedly other denominations too, seems to have no real answer to this critical situation; if indeed it is even understood or appreciated as critical. It has, with other denominations, tied itself wholeheartedly (i.e. constitutionally, financially and from the point of view of stationing its ministers) to a form of church life which, though once reasonably relevant and successful, is now far too static and localized to attract or hold a mobile and increasingly cosmopolitan society. The consequences are, amongst other things, an ageing membership,[15] the loss of thousands of younger members each year and the ever present spectacle of half-used or redundant churches.

Of course there will remain many locals in modern society for whom the local pattern of Methodist congregational life *may* have some attraction. It is conceivable that our society could again become more local and less cosmopolitan in orientation, and of course there are other factors leading to a decline in churchgoing besides that of 'cultural lag'. But it would not be an exaggeration to say that unless the church seriously and urgently tackles the problem of reshaping its locally oriented life and witness into a more cosmopolitan pattern, there may not be much left to shape by the close of this century.

NOTES

1. M. Young and P. Willmott, *Family and Kinship in East London* (revised edition), Penguin Books 1962.

R. Frankenberg, *Village on the Border*, Cohen and West 1957.

H. Jennings, *Societies in the Making*, Routledge and Kegan Paul 1962.

W. M. Williams, *Gosforth*, Routledge and Kegan Paul 1956.

2. J. Klein, *Samples from English Cultures* Vol. I, Routledge and Kegan Paul 1965.

R. Frankenberg, *Communities in Britain*, Penguin Books 1966.

D. B. Clark, *Community and a Suburban Village* (unpublished Ph.D. thesis), University of Sheffield 1969.

3. M. Stacey, *Tradition and Change*, OUP 1960.

4. M. Stacey, op. cit., pp. 167–68.

5. M. Stacey, op. cit., p. 158.

6. T. Brennan, E. W. Cooney and H. Pollins, *Social Change in South-West Wales*, Watts and Co. 1954.

7. J. M. Mogey, *Family and Neighbourhood*, OUP 1956.

8. N. Elias and J. L. Scotson, *The Established and the Outsiders*, Cass and Co. 1965.

9. F. Tönnies, *Community and Association* (translated and supplemented by Loomis, C. P.), Routledge and Kegan Paul 1955 (first published 1887).

10. M. Stacey, op. cit., pp. 178–82.

11. R. K. Merton, *Social Theory and Social Structure* (revised edition), Collier-Macmillan 1957, pp. 387–420.

12. J. K. Perraton, 'Community Planning–An Analysis of Certain Social Aims' *J. Town Planning Inst.* Vol. 53, No. 3 (pp. 95–98) March 1967.

13. Figures relating to the Oakcroft population as a whole were obtained from the 1961 General Census.

14. J. Klein, op. cit., p. 95.

15. For statistics portraying the ageing and declining membership in the Bristol, and Manchester and Stockport Districts see J. Butler and B. Jones, *A Statistical Analysis of Methodist Membership in Two Areas of England* (unpublished), 1969.

5 Religion in Rural Norfolk

Peter D. Varney

Introduction

The area of Norfolk described in this article is the geographical region of South Norfolk which lies on a plateau to the south of Norwich, and is approximately 25 miles from east to west and 15 miles from north to south. The population of the 79 civil parishes in South Norfolk when this study was made in 1962 was 44,835.

Two-thirds of the region is arable land. The traditional agricultural pattern of intensive mixed farming with river valley pasturing remains, but market gardening, fruit growing and poultry enterprises have been developed more recently. The area includes several small towns which provide shopping and other facilities and have industries closely related to agriculture. The parishes near Norwich have increasing dormitory populations but the more isolated parishes have decreasing populations.

Manner of life is the chief determinant of social status in South Norfolk, and traditional loyalty to established institutions, including the Church of England, remains. The Conservative party receives solid support from the majority of the region's electorate.

The religious history of the region has been similar to other parts of southern England. After the Reformation the Elizabethan settlement was leniently enforced in South Norfolk, and independent congregations, which often included anabaptists, were founded. By the seventeenth century puritanism had spread within the Church of England and the number of Independent and Baptist congregations had also increased. For two centuries after the Restoration latitudinarianism was widespread in the Established Church and Norwich was popularly known as the 'Dead See'. In 1790 the Wesleys visited the region and during the following century Methodist 'societies' were established in a quarter of the region's parishes. At the end of the nineteenth century the high church movement spread to a number of parishes and, like their evangelical predecessors, the high churchmen helped in the restoration of the Church of England's sense of mission.

Religious life in the South Norfolk region

All the major Christian denominations are represented in South Norfolk. Questionnaires were sent to all places of worship in the region and the table, which is based on the replies to the questionnaire, shows that well over half the places of worship are Anglican, and almost a quarter are Methodist. Many of the buildings of the Methodist and other non-Anglican Protestant denominations are very small and their proportion of the total on church membership rolls is only half their proportion of the places of worship.

In South Norfolk the Church of England stands out as the Established Church of the nation, while in contrast within the Methodist Church, and especially in its village societies, there is a strong feeling of a people set apart by their denominational allegiance. Of the major denominations Baptists and some Congregationalists are the most exclusive but the Brethren and Pentecostal Assemblies in the region are even more exclusive.

All except two of the region's civil parishes have at least one Anglican church. The rural strength of Methodism is reflected in the location of its societies in both small and large villages as well as in the towns. The other denominations are mainly based in the towns where they draw congregations from a wide area. The table shows that the membership rolls of the churches in the region include 8,778 persons, equal to one-fifth of the total population of South Norfolk; 15·6% of the population are on Anglican rolls, compared with only 6·3% in all England in 1962.[2] Individual Anglican churches have a larger number of people on their membership rolls than all except the Roman Catholic churches. The average Methodist church roll is the smallest because of the many small village societies. The high Roman Catholic figure is based on the number of Easter confessions and it includes some adherents who live outside the region.

The religious personnel are almost equally divided between the full-time clergy, who total 113 in all the denominations, and the 130 regular lay-workers. Over half the Anglican priests have charge of two churches, which is nearly twice the national proportion, and only a third of the parishes are under the sole charge of one priest. In Methodist and Baptist churches lay leaders more often take worship

DENOMINATIONAL MEMBERSHIP
AND CHURCH ATTENDANCE

Denomination	No. of Churches	%	Member-ship Roll	%	Total Average Attendance on:			
					Sundays	%	Festivals	%
Anglican	94	61·0	6,754	76·9	4,387	61·9	9,805	66·1
average per church			72		47		104	
Methodist	35	22·7	921	10·5	1,172	16·5	2,515	17·0
average per church			29		33		72	
Baptist	8	5·2	255	2·9	333	4·7	660	4·4
average per church			32		42		85	
Other Denominations	13	8·4	435	5·0	705	9·9	1,250	8·4
average per church			33		54		96	
Roman Catholic	4	2·6	413	4·7	494	7·0	605	4·1
average per church			103		124		151	
Total	154		8,778		7,091		14,835	
average per church			57		46		96	
Percentage of population of South Norfolk			19·6		15·8		33·1	

than their ordained ministers, who each have to serve many congregations. The majority of the region's clergy are engaged in full-time pastoral work, although most of the pastors of the smaller denominations are part-time. Over half the lay-workers in South Norfolk are Methodist local preachers, most of whom take services regularly. Less than one-fifth of the lay-workers are Anglicans, and they include the members of a religious community. There are 1,940 other voluntary lay officials who include 1,234 members of Anglican parochial church councils.

In rural Norfolk denominational interaction has been much less than in other parts of England. Non-Anglicans may expect to be visited by the Church of England priest and to attend the parish church on occasions of national importance but few Anglicans desire to worship in any other church. Changes of denomination occur most frequently at marriage, especially when one of the partners is a Roman Catholic. Geographical reasons may lead people to attend a church of a different denomination, and one person interviewed, a member of the Church of Scotland, has become a temporary communicant at his parish church. United services of Anglican, Roman Catholic and Free Churches have been held at times of national thanksgiving, and during the week of prayer for Christian unity in the past few years, and in a few parishes there are joint prayer and study groups and a regular interchange of preachers. There are some exclusivist congregations in all the major churches and these, together with the Brethren and Pentecostals, have remained outside the developments in Christian co-operation. There has been considerable overlapping in charitable work until recently when fund raising, for Christian Aid and Oxfam, has brought together members of nearly all the churches, including the Roman Catholics.

The information about church attendance and other religious activities obtained from the questionnaire is shown on the table and map. About one-sixth of the population of South Norfolk regularly attend Sunday worship and the proportion rises to a third on festivals. Although three-quarters of the total church members are Anglicans they make up only 61·9% of the worshippers on ordinary Sundays. The average Anglican attendance at each service on an ordinary Sunday is 25, but it rises to 71 on occasions such as Christmas or Harvest Festival. Although the Methodists make up only one-tenth of the total church members one-sixth of the total Sunday attendance is at their churches. The average size of their congregations at each service is 21. In all the Free Churches attendances on a Church Anniversary Sunday are greatly increased by visitors from other churches.

The number of people who attend more than one Sunday service varies with each denomination. Where there is a resident Anglican priest an early celebration of holy communion is normally held: a total of 772 persons attend this and often another service later in

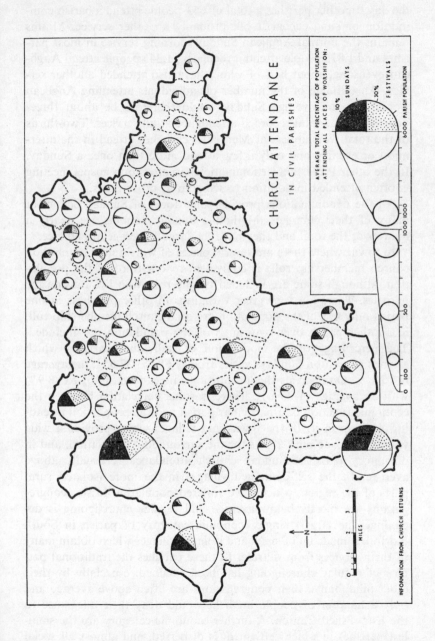

CHURCH ATTENDANCE
IN CIVIL PARISHES

AVERAGE TOTAL PERCENTAGE OF POPULATION
ATTENDING ALL PLACES OF WORSHIP ON:

10% SUNDAYS

30% FESTIVALS

6000 PARISH POPULATION

INFORMATION FROM CHURCH RETURNS

MILES

the day. In other parishes a total of 663 people attend a parish communion or sung eucharist but probably no other service. Matins remains the normal Anglican Sunday morning service in most parishes and 1,876 people attend it regularly; 1,345 people attend Anglican evensong, about half of whom have also attended another service. An estimate of the number of individuals attending Anglican worship on an average Sunday would therefore be about three-quarters of the total recorded attendance at all services. Two-thirds of the total worshippers at Methodist churches attend in the afternoon or evening and only a few attend more than once a Sunday. In the other Protestant denominations an afternoon gospel meeting is often attended in addition to worship at other times.

All the denominations provide some form of Sunday School at many of their churches, Methodist Sunday Schools are nearly a quarter of the total and they have the largest average attendance.

In towns where there are several places of worship the number on church membership rolls is equivalent to one-third of the population, although some are included on the rolls who live outside the parishes. There are very great variations in other parishes; in one parish only 4% of the population are on a church membership roll, in another parish over two-thirds of the population are included. The percentage of the population of individual parishes which attends church on Sundays varies from 3·6% to 37·6%; the average is 15·8%. On festivals the proportion ranges from 3·4% to 88·9% with an average of 33·1%. There is some correlation between the economic function of a particular parish and the proportion attending worship in it. In the towns and villages which provide a wide variety of economic services for the surrounding population, and in dormitory parishes, Sunday church attendance is usually above average. In the self-contained villages in the more isolated rural parts of the region, which have suffered population losses, congregations are mostly below average and regular churchgoing is declining. The largest single economic category of parish in South Norfolk is made up of small and isolated villages which obtain many of their services from outside. In these parishes the traditional pattern of regular churchgoing has been retained, especially by their older inhabitants, their congregations are often above average and only a handful of people in them would deny their allegiance to the Established Church. A further economic category are the smallest parishes in which settlement is dispersed, and almost all social

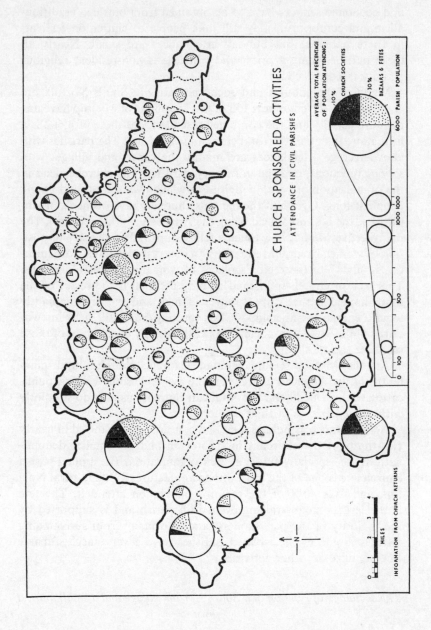

CHURCH SPONSORED ACTIVITIES

ATTENDANCE IN CIVIL PARISHES

AVERAGE TOTAL PERCENTAGE OF POPULATION ATTENDING:

10% CHURCH SOCIETIES

30% BAZAARS & FETES

6000 PARISH POPULATION

1000 1000

500

100

0

MILES

INFORMATION FROM CHURCH RETURNS

N

and economic services have to be obtained from outside. Traditionalism and conformism may still take people to church on festivals in these parishes, but Sunday attendances are small. Nearly all these parishes share a priest and when he is non-resident religious activity rapidly declines.

Many of the cultural and social activities in South Norfolk are sponsored by the churches: 133 of the 154 places of worship have one or more activity and the combined attendance at these of 4,662 is a little more than half the total church membership. The parishes with above-average attendances are mainly the towns and villages with service functions, and the dormitory parishes. The churches lead in the organization of youth activities to which over a thousand young people belong. Over half the region's churches have women's organizations, the best organized being the Anglican Mothers' Union. The many active Methodist women's fellowships reflect the strong position of women in rural Methodism. In contrast to women's organizations only 17 of the region's places of worship have men's groups. This lack of church-sponsored activity for men is the result of the more limited leisure opportunities of men and the predominantly female church membership. 'Class meetings' are still held in two-thirds of the Methodist societies and attended by over a third of those on these societies' rolls.

All the Methodist and Roman Catholic churches and nine-tenths of the Anglican churches make available some kind of publication to their members; the Anglican churches usually do so jointly with other parishes in their deanery.

Activities such as jumble sales and concerts are organized in nearly two-thirds of the churches in the region and the smaller denominations are especially active in their organization. The annual parish church fete is one of the most important features of life in rural Norfolk and over 40% of the region's population attend it. The fete is the largest money-raising event in a parish and is supported by the majority of the parishioners, and also many from surrounding villages. Some of the isolated parishes have a very successful fete but organize no other activities.

The sociology of religion in a South Norfolk village and a small market town

A detailed study has been made of two representative parishes in

South Norfolk based on interviews with a sample of their population. The first parish, A, lies in an area south of Norwich where there has been a steady increase in population since 1931. It is a village with a good range of service facilities, including a dozen shops, a voluntary primary school and Anglican, Methodist and Strict Baptist churches. The parish includes a small council housing estate and a new private estate. Parish B is a small market town and minor communications centre a little further from Norwich. Since 1951 its population has grown at a rate above the regional average but much of the area included within the parish boundaries remains rural. Close to its main street are two well-designed local authority housing estates and farther away there is new private housing, both developments blending happily with the older buildings in the centre of this attractive country town.[4] There are a good range of facilities including Anglican, Methodist and Roman Catholic churches, a secondary school, banks, insurance offices and a few light industries. In parish A the population in 1961 was 695 persons and in parish B it was 1,242. Ten per cent of the electorate were chosen for interview but questions were also asked of those interviewed about the people living in their households, so that information was collected for about one-quarter of the population of the two parishes.

An analysis of the population of the two parishes by the type of industry in which people work shows that the largest single category is made up of those in agriculture.[5] Distributive and other services also employ over a third of the total in both parishes. In the town parish a larger proportion of the remainder are employed in transport and manufacturing. About a third of those employed in both parishes work outside them, especially in Norwich, and both have many women working seasonally or occasionally in agriculture. Both parishes have a similar proportion of the people interviewed in the professional classes and in the category of low-grade non-manual workers.[6] In parish A a greater proportion of the population are in the higher grade non-manual classes, and in the town parish, B, the skilled manual category is better represented. Both the parishes have a considerable number in the unskilled manual class, many of whom are farm labourers.

More people in parish A hold higher educational qualifications and in a cultural classification made on the basis of style of living, speech and vocabulary the village parish also has a larger proportion in the higher categories. The town parish offers more social activities and a higher proportion of people there are regularly engaged in them but in parish A the new immigrants, who have few personal links with the parish when they arrive, are also active in social activities.

In the town parish the majority of voters intended to support the two major political parties; 43·1% would have supported the Conservatives, 37·5% Labour, and 19% the Liberals. In the village parish 45·9% said they would vote Conservative and the Labour and Liberal parties were each supported by 27%. At the time of the interviews, in 1962, there had been a national increase in support for the Liberal party and insufficient evidence was obtained in the two parishes to determine whether members of the Methodist or other Free Churches would usually support the Liberals in greater proportion than Anglicans. In the town parish a significantly greater proportion of non-Anglicans than Anglicans said they would support the Labour party.

About four-fifths of the population of both parishes are Anglicans[7] but the proportion of Methodists in the town parish, 15·1%, is nearly twice that in parish A. Just over 2% in both parishes say they have no religious allegiance. The regular congregations in all the churches contain a majority of old people and the vitality that younger adults could bring to church life is therefore lost. In parish A members of the new professions in the 30–49 age group and those over 65 are numerically the most important groups of weekly attenders but in parish B people over 50 predominate. The proportion of weekly attenders aged between 15 and 29 in both parishes is much less than the proportion of the total population in this age group.

When social class indices are used to examine the membership of the denominations it is clear that the most active members tend to be from the higher social classes, especially in the village parish. The largest proportion of weekly attenders in this parish are in the higher grade non-manual class, so that people like managers, executives and professionals are most likely to be regular churchgoers. In contrast in the same parish less than one-sixth of the weekly attenders come from the semi-skilled and unskilled manual groups, although these groups make up nearly half the total informants. In the town parish, however, just under three-quarters of the weekly attenders are in the manually employed group, which is almost equal to their proportion of the total informants.

About a third of the people interviewed can be considered as active members of their denominations: they are full members of their church by confirmation or its equivalent and are also either on a membership roll or are church officials. Most of the remainder are baptized and confirmed but are only nominal adherents of their denomination. The Anglican Church, as expected, has the largest proportion of nominal adherents, almost 70% in both parishes.

About three-quarters of the people interviewed in both parishes say they belong to their denomination because it is the one of their upbringing. Only nine of the 107 Anglicans interviewed have changed their denominational allegiance, but six of the remaining 18 informants now belong to denominations different from their parents.

The harvest festival has a special place in the life of the two parishes and it attracts over half their total population. Up to four-fifths of the informants and their households attend church on other special occasions. A slightly smaller proportion of the total attend church only for rites of passage, such as the baptism or wedding of a friend. Those who say they attend church regularly every Sunday in the year make up exactly the same proportion, one-sixth of the total, in both parishes. A much smaller proportion of the Anglicans than of the other denominations are weekly attenders. In contrast over a third of the Methodists in the two parishes attend weekly, a proportion which is considerably above the average.

The most important social activities of the churches are their organizations for particular groups of their members, such as the Anglican Mothers' Union. Women's organizations at all the churches are best supported and over a fifth of the women in both parishes belong to them. In contrast only 4% of adult males belong to any church organization. Youth groups include a fifth of those under 21 in parish A and twice this proportion in parish B. A church-sponsored old people's organization, to which nearly 10% of the retired population belong, and a small study group are also organized in parish B. Those who attend church bazaars and concerts are usually active members of their church but the annual summer fete, in aid of the parish church funds, and in parish B for the Methodist church also, are attended by over half the population.

The informants showed very little reluctance to talk about the extent of their more personal religious activities. Even amongst those who do not attend church the saying of prayers is widespread, and about half those interviewed say they pray daily. The depth of individual religious life may also be assessed by the frequency of bible reading, which a quarter of the informants in both parishes do either daily or weekly. An individual's interest in religion is also shown by the amount of religious programmes he watches on television or hears on the radio. In parish A 81·3% and in parish B 48·9% say they hear or see such programmes, either daily or weekly, and most of these are people who only occasionally attend church worship.

In parish A over half the informants say they are visited monthly or more often by their parish priest or minister, but in parish B less than a quarter say they are regularly visited and a third say they never receive visits. This difference is partly explained by the fact that parish A has only half the number of parishioners as the other parish. In the town parish visiting is also made more difficult because more adults are working during the day. Some of the regular church-goers think of the parish priest primarily as a visitor to themselves but more regard him as having a wide pastoral concern for all the people in his charge.

An attempt was also made to examine the attitudes of informants towards the main doctrines of Christian belief. In both parishes only about a third of those interviewed are able to give any reasoned explanation of their belief in God, although more accept the belief without explanation or question. Although the informants in parish A have a 'higher' social and cultural level no more of them are able to offer an explanation of their belief in God. Nearly a quarter of the informants in both parishes say that they are undecided or uncertain about the existence of God. A greater proportion of the weekly attenders are able to give a reasoned explanation, but a considerable proportion of them can still offer no definite opinion. The informants' attitudes to the sacraments, other denominations, the difference they feel their religious beliefs make to them and changes in the forms of worship also indicate great uncertainty about their religion and it would seem that in both parishes little information has been given to them, or retained by them, about basic Christian beliefs.

Conclusion

In an area of rural England like South Norfolk traditional social institutions, including the established Church of England, still receive strong support. Evidence of this support can be found in the large attendances at the harvest festival and at the parish church fete. On both these occasions the church is supported as a part of the traditional life of the parish and those who attend may have no strong allegiance to the church and only a superficial knowledge of Christian belief. On a more personal level, however, although religious commitment is not expressed by regular church-going, it is revealed in the habit of regular private prayer, which more than half the informants in the two selected parishes observe.

NOTES

1. This paper is based on a thesis entitled 'The Social Anthropology of a Region in Southern Norfolk with Special Reference to Religious Life', presented for the degree of M.A., University of Durham, 1964. The field work for this study was carried out in 1962 and the statistics and text refer to that year.

2. *Facts and Figures about the Church of England: No. 3.*, Central Board of Finance of the Church of England, London 1965, p. 58, table 71.

3. Ibid., p. 16, table 11.

4. An editorial in the *Eastern Daily Press*, 19 October 1963, described this parish as 'a community of modern houses and a secondary modern school which is a demonstration that it is still possible . . . for a country town to grow delight-fully'.

5. Forty per cent of the working population in the village parish A, and 31·9% in the town parish B, are employed in agriculture.

6. Social classes have been determined according to the criteria proposed by J. Hall and D. Caradog Jones in 'The Social Grading of Occupations', *British Journal of Sociology*, Vol. 1, No. 1, March 1950, pp.31–55.

7. In parish A 88·3% of the population state they are Anglicans, in parish B 77·9%.

6 Sunday Observance and Social Class

Roger Homan

IT IS the purpose of this essay to establish that the evolution of Sunday over the last 120 years has been a progression towards the achievement, not yet realized, of a right balance of divergent class interests. The argument will develop through three phases, seeking to show:

1. that the norms and values relating to the use of Sunday have been largely determined by elements within the middle class;
2. that the institutions and structures which these norms and values are calculated to support either have been contrary to the interests of the working class or else were not within the reach of its members;
3. that the working class has either accepted these norms and has emulated the middle class or else it has rejected them, attempting to establish its own norms and values.

It will emerge from this examination that the composition of the groups and organizations involved in the conflict have not at all been confined to the social strata one would expect; notwithstanding, there has always been a powerful element of class consciousness. The campaigns have been seen by the liberals and radicals within the framework of a class struggle, but the notion that the pressure for a strict observance of Sunday has come exclusively from the middle and upper levels of society or that they were all working people who wanted to relax Sunday observance, is a theory that does not stand up to close examination; the notion has been developed and popularized by political slogans, and it is quite the opposite that is the finding of the present investigation.

In the nineteenth century, it has been said, popular radicalism was 'the product of the leisure of Saturday night and Sunday morning, the pothouse and the chapel, not of the working week'.[1] That the day and a half of leisure placed at the disposal of the ordinary

people by the 1847 Factory Act was the subject of considerable contention between the classes will be frequently evident in this essay.
But it will also become clear that an analysis of the social structure
according to class is not entirely helpful; we encounter in any study
of the Sabbath question a number of groups each consisting of individuals of rather different occupations and economic status. Neither radicalism nor traditionalism, neither established religion nor
nonconformity are to be seen as purely class phenomena; and because
there are those among the lower orders of society who passively
accept the values of the middle classes, we find that the groups of
sabbatarians are as heterogeneous as those of the abolitionists.

The radicals have been particularly guilty of creating the stereotype which this article attempts to break; in identifying themselves
with what they conceived to be the interests of the working classes,
they forced the sabbatarians into an identity with the affluent members of society who were, if the stereotype is to be believed, denying
to those whom they oppressed the opportunities of leisure on Sunday that they so richly enjoyed during the week. As a description
of the real situation this was an oversimplification, but there was
evidence that fitted it very well. The belief that the riot was conventionally an instrument of working-class pressure may lead us to
suppose with Marx that the 1855 disturbances in Hyde Park were
the activities of labouring men,[2] whereas it appears that drink
sellers[3] and members of the clerical and professional classes[4] were
prominently involved too. A crowd composed entirely of working
people would not have won much sympathy,[5] while these demonstrations were in principle supported by the respectable press in
which it was observed that those taking part were making a genuine
complaint.[6] The Lord's Day Observance Society attracted very few
aristocrats and, in the other extreme, potential members from the
working class were effectively excluded by the annual subscription
which stood at ten shillings in 1840;[7] such working-class allegiance
as the society managed to secure was on the strength of its assur-
ance of a six-day working week. Nor did the Working Men's Lord's
Day Rest Association contrast as sharply with the predominantly
middle-class membership of the LDOS as its name might lead us to
expect. It was formed by the amalgamation of a number of local
genuinely working men's Sabbath conservation societies, with an
annual membership fee of about one shilling; but within 40 years
it lost its grass roots hierarchy and in 1895 its secretary reported

that of 1,648 subscriptions, 592 were from ladies and 156 from clergy and that 'the working people are not accustomed to give much money to objects of this sort, and although they value their Sunday, yet we could not carry on our work vigorously unless we had got the support of others'.[8] The National Sunday League, which campaigned for various measures to be taken relaxing Sunday observance and came into direct and deliberate conflict over these issues with the Lord's Day Observance Society, was composed of a 'mixture of plebeian and professional class radicals'.[9] There was therefore a considerable class mixture in both sabbatarian and anti-sabbatarian parties, and to suggest that sabbatarians belonged entirely to the middle class is to exaggerate what admittedly existed as a general tendency. Notwithstanding, the radicals were quick to assert that this was the case; however unjustified the analysis may be that identifies the sabbatarian cause with that of the upper strata of society, it is important to notice that it was as an inter-class conflict that the Sabbath question was understood by those involved in the continuing debate. The person who at a meeting of the Islington Sunday League in 1873 shouted at the secretary of the Lord's Day Observance Society 'You're not a working man'[10] was expressing a very general attitude towards sabbatarians. Sometimes it worked the other way too; in one of many tracts on the subject to be written in the 1850s a Banbury sabbatarian minister, Joseph Parker, referred to Sunday excursionists as 'the laziest, dirtyest, poorest and silliest of the working classes'.[11]

The identification of the middle class with churchgoing and the respectable use of Sunday need not be argued;[12] the puritan discipline which inspired the rigours of Victorian sabbatarianism was deeply conscious of its function to preserve middle-class values such as respectability[13] and the Evangelicals of the late eighteenth century who, by identifying Sunday with the Jewish Sabbath, were able to give to the nation acceptable (that is, Scriptural) authority for the institution that was of their making[14] were predominantly middle and upper class; they fortified themselves with developed biblical theology[15] and those who for social and humanitarian reasons wanted to set about a reform of the Christian sabbath without dispensing of it altogether had first to contend with the arguments made in its defence by numerous religious tracts.[16]

The Marxist plausibly argues that the churches are the means whereby bourgeois values are imposed on the proletariat. Breaking

up a Carlisle sabbatarian meeting in 1839, G. J. Harney claimed that
the sabbatarian rule was 'fear God, honour the Queen and work
for your tyrants'.[17] Charles Booth gives three accounts of the working-class Sunday in London, and each follows the same pattern:
rise late, wait for the public house to open, return home when it
closes at 3 o'clock, lunch, sleep, and perhaps go again to the public
house in the evening;[18] the most notable omissions in the churchgoer's Sunday are the visits to the public house, and meals are earlier
to fit in with the times of services.[19] Internalization is probably the
most effective means of securing conformity among the working
people, but the great numbers of the respected groups in society
who were ostentatious in their observance made a deep impression
upon those who noticed them. Less subtly, the Lord's Day Observance Society offered prizes for essays on the Sunday question written by working men.[20] As early as 1798 'it was a wonder to the
lower orders throughout all parts of England, to see the avenues to
the churches filled with carriages. This novel appearance prompted
the simple country people to enquire what was the matter'.[21] Those
who so paraded were the men and women for whom these 'simple
people' worked and whose example they were wont to follow.
What appeared to be the generally accepted code was an equal
if not greater pressure to conform in Wales, where a Cardiganshire
villager told one investigator, 'I'm not religious by any means but
the least we can do is not to break the Sabbath.'[22] The religious observance of Sunday is thus extended to involve the co-operation of
working people, religious, non-religious and indifferent; it is a question of respect.

The norms of nineteenth-century sabbatarianism may be expressed in terms of society's expectations of the individual, therefore; he should attend church or chapel at least once on a Sunday;
he will wear his 'Sunday best'; he must abstain from secular enter-
tainments; he must spend the day in religious conversation and
thought and in the performance of certain good works; he must
confine his reading to suitable literature, much of which was
produced for the purpose; he would not show himself in public
save on his way to worship or in the course of his permitted afternoon
walk; he was not to be involved in Sunday trade, nor should he use
public transport on a Sunday; he should do his best to use the day
to elevate his kin in the consideration of Christian matters.[23] Such a
Sunday was more easily observed and enjoyed by the family with

its own conveyance and household staff than by the people who lived away from the fresh air and open spaces, had no transport, were not paid until late on a Saturday night, and lacked the respectable clothing and domestic comforts of their social superiors.

If the prosperous were by their part in the Evangelical Revival responsible for establishing the Victorian Sunday with all its restraints, they were also more responsible than the working classes for relaxing these austerities in the second half of the century; the reform is more the doing of middle-class liberalism than of working-class pressure. In Wales, where the humble and poor identified themselves with conservative Nonconformity, they resisted this liberalism.[24] But in England there was from the middle of the century a growing interest and concern for the underprivileged masses living in the industrial towns; until 1848 the churches and the legislature had spoken with one voice, and their divergence dates from the time when statute began to recognize the needs of the working people.[25] The decline of the Victorian Sunday only really got under way when the ruling and governing classes started to fall away from the church[26] and the upper classes are blamed by the clergy for popularizing Sunday as a day of leisure, which they did by exercising themselves on their bicycles.[27] While the case for the rigorous observance of Sunday was initially supported on theological grounds, the opposition to it has been generally utilitarian, in consequence of which the justification of such observance tends now to be based on a social rather than religious foundation.[28] The current literature of the Lord's Day Observance Society sometimes argues from Scripture and other times appeals to common sense, attempting to prove that God's law on the subject is reasonable. The LDOS publication *100 Facts you should know about the Lord's Day* includes 45 sentences that refer to the bible, 42 from the Fathers and the Reformers and other statements that could be described as theological, and 13 'facts' that appeal to reason; of these last are 'The sabbath strengthens family ties', 'It promotes all that is highest and best in man' and 'It safeguards the interest of the workman'.[29]

The 1854 Wilson–Patten Act closed drinking places on Sundays to withdraw the temptation from the working classes who were 'very much in the condition of children';[30] a statute with such an expressed motive represents a transitional stage between legislation which is manifestly in the interests of the middle class and that which is in accord with the wishes of the working people and not, that is, what the ruling classes regard as good for them. Previously there had been cases where the habits of the rich were protected and their servants were obliged to co-operate by working in order that their employers might be served. In 1840 the High Constable of Brighton recommended to agreeing magistrates that carriagemen should only be allowed to ply for hire outside churches on a Sunday when the weather was inclement.[31] Such subordination of the workers to the whim of the social élite is seen again four years later when Parliament had to consider a Bill which would have provided on Sundays at least one stopping train on each railway line with a third class fare of one penny per mile; the Bishop of London opposed the Bill and all such Sunday rail services. If the Bill had been rejected the rich could still have travelled by rail during the week but the poor who had no such free time would have been deprived of the opportunity.[32] More recently, in 1923, the LCC Park Committee recommended to the LCC that permission be granted to certain athletic clubs to play games on Sundays in Hainault Forest and other open spaces. A strong religious objection that this would involve the Sunday labour of two park-keepers forced the Park committee to withdraw its recommendation. Those who argued that 'The sabbath was made for man, not man for the sabbath' saw that the need for the young people of London to play in open spaces was indeed great and were highly critical of the small sector which wanted to impose its day of gloom on the rest of the population.[33] It was not taken into account that the poor by nature spent their leisure time in public, and those who would deprive them of their traditional forms of recreation without providing any alternative than church-going were deeply resented.

There was the same conflict where Sunday trading was concerned. Much of the business that was done on this day was between the working-class family and the small shopkeeper. Marx complained that the Sunday Trading Bill of 1855 hit only the small shopkeepers as the big stores with a middle-class trade did not open on Sunday in any case.[34] This is also the finding of Caradog-Jones[35] and the report of a parish priest in Portsmouth;[36] and in Booth's London the working-class housewife made her way to the street market on Sunday morning.[37] Working people, furthermore, believed that goods were cheaper on Sunday.[38] When Lord Robert Grosvenor, the man behind the Sunday Trading Bill, was challenged that it was directed solely against the poor, he is reported to have replied that 'the aristocracy was largely refraining from employing its horses and servants on Sundays';[39] the nobility is supposed to have walked to church.[40]

The divergence of class interests is also manifest in the question of Sunday labour. Sir Andrew Agnew's Bill of 1833 laid down 'that it is the bounden duty of the legislature to protect every class of society against being compelled to sacrifice their comfort, health, religious privileges, and conscience, for the convenience, enjoyment or supposed advantage of any other class on the Lord's Day . . . except menial servants acting in the necessary service of their employers'.[41] The last clause, of course, may be interpreted to the liking of the employer, and along with others of its kind was responsible for the ultimate rejection of the Bill. It is clear that the rules which preserved a quiet and restful day for the rich did no such thing for the poor, whose leisure had often to be given up. It was in order to extend to the working people some of the facilities that the rich were able to enjoy that the National Sunday League was formed in 1875.

The Sunday opening of museums and art galleries, which was sought after by the League, was made an issue in the 1885 election campaign, when one Member of Parliament, C. A. V. Conybeare, wrote somewhat satirically: 'I have ever advocated the proposal [to open museums] in the interests of true religion . . . I, for one, am fully persuaded that to give these poorly-housed and hard-worked toilers the opportunity of beholding, on a Sunday afternoon, a grand picture of the Virgin and her Child, or the Saviour on the Cross, or of reaching some volume containing noble and elevating thoughts [or] the contemplation for half an hour on the Sabbath day of the Raphael cartoons in the South Kensington Museum . . . would be at least as likely to convert a heathen mind as a long sermon on the doctrine of the Trinity.[42] As the writer reminds us by his dedicated profession of the opposite view, those things which the middle class appreciated and enjoyed were often meaningless to the less culturally aware working class, whose real pleasures were perhaps to be derived from lighter forms of recreation. When the 1847 Factory Act provided working men with a half-day holiday on Saturday, they did not make their way to museums and art galleries but queued for football matches.[43] The class of literature considered appropriate for Sunday reading was also above the level of their interest.[44] One of many anonymous pamphleteers of the mid-nineteenth century suggested, in an aside, that perhaps the working people were barren of elevated thoughts; in a passage in which he considers that there is one law for the rich and another for the poor, he asks: 'What can the poor hackney-coachman think, if he reflect at all, of the religion of those who employ him to exercise his ordinary calling, in open violation of the laws of his country and of the fourth commandment?'[45]

The controversy concerned with the right use of Sunday was for a long time preoccupied with the reasons for its observance and not with its effects, and this first concern was not changed until the basis for a literal interpretation of Scripture was undermined by biblical scholars; simultaneously, liberal theologians learned from the advent of social work that it was time to draw attention to the ethical content of their faith. Formerly, if the bible said you were not to work, it mattered not that you should go hungry by keeping the commandment. The middle classes were happy with and derived benefit from a rigorous observance; they were able to spend their day in pleasant reflection. Too often the houses of the poor were the good reason why they wanted Sunday excursions and outdoor activities; but public facilities were denied them by those who had no personal need for them, and the poor were obliged to abstain. The provision of churches in industrial areas was not good because they would not have been patronized and pew rents were often effective discriminators against the poor. Brighton, for instance, at the end of the eighteenth century had one parish church, and two or three chapels established by the Prince Regent for his own use, for his guests at the Royal Pavilion, and for others of their kind. H. Hamilton Maughan, a historian of Brighton churches, tells us: 'Such chapels, being unashamedly of the nature of a financial enterprise, reserved their ministrations for the fashionable and well-to-do, upon whose patronage their success, and even their existence, depended.'[46] Though Brighton was an extreme case – not every town being attended by the aristocracy in great numbers – exclusion of the poor by pew rents, which the Tractarians set about abolishing, was not only here an important feature of class discrimination operating within the church. There is still today a tendency in rural areas for the morning service to be attended by the local gentry and the evening service by the ordinary people, a practice which originated when those of modest circumstances were engaged during the morning in the households of the rich and only the landlords were free to attend.[47]

By the middle of the nineteenth century the alienation of the social classes was particularly acute and was frequently evident in discussion of the Sunday question. On Sunday, 24 June 1855, the Chartists held their first demonstration against the Sunday Trading Bill that was being sponsored by Lord Robert Grosvenor, to which reference has already been made. The poster advertising the meeting is particularly relevant to this present discussion. It was circulated in London during the week preceding the Sunday and read as follows:

New Sunday Bill prohibiting newspapers, shaving, smoking, eating and drinking and all kinds of recreation and nourishment, both corporal and spiritual, which the poor people still enjoy at the present time. An open-air meeting of artisans, workers and 'the lower orders' generally of the capital will take place in Hyde Park on Sunday afternoon to see how religiously the aristocracy is observing the Sabbath and how anxious it is not to employ its servants and horses on that day, as Lord Robert Grosvenor said in his speech ... Come and bring your wives and children in order that they may profit by the example their 'betters' set them.[48]

The passive solution is total acceptance of middle-class norms. The working man rises to the spirit of the day, dresses up in his Sunday best and marks the day by a special decorum in his behaviour. One day in seven he lives out of his class; swearing and gambling are worse sins on the Sabbath than on a week-day because they are not condoned by the social class whose values take effect from Saturday midnight. This passive acceptance is best seen where Nonconformity has successfully involved the working class, as it has with the working people of Wales and Scotland. 'The Welsh working man' reports E. T. Davies, 'rouses himself. . . . It is his best chance, all the week through, of showing himself in his own character. He marks his sense of it by a suit of clothes hardly less sabbatical than the day itself. . . . They always seem to be better dressed on a Sunday than the same classes in England.'[49] He looks to 'respectable' groups within his society for a sense of what is proper. The association of Sunday with high standards of behaviour was also made a few years ago by the late Archbishop Garbett of York: 'If the cinemas are open on Sunday, let them show the best and not the second-rate films.'[50] The respectable observance of Sunday has been a more natural practice for the people of rural areas than for their urban counterparts: 'Life in the peaceful country village, with its many disadvantages, did certainly offer more opportunities of cultivating the higher nature, wherever the inclination was present. Generally speaking, the labourer had no desire to forsake the traditions of his forefathers who slept in the little churchyard.'[51]

Alternatively, middle-class norms and values may be rejected. The working-class groups may determine their own codes and abide by these. Perhaps they are forced to this out of circumstance: the Report on Mines of 1842 states that many women and girls were so physically exhausted by their six days work that they had to spend Sunday in bed.[52] At the same time a letter appeared in the *Morning Chronicle* from a Hinckley stockinger who quoted the defence of sabbath breaking made by an illiterate colleague on whose behalf he was writing:

> Look at my children and my home and ask no more: I will tell you, however, why I work on this day. It is because my poverty compels me; I *cannot* and *will* not hear my children cry for bread without taking the only means honestly to get it. Last Monday morning I rose at two o'clock and worked till near midnight. I rose at six o'clock each succeeding morning and worked until between eleven and twelve each night, and now you see what I have for dinner. I cannot do it longer. I shall go to an untimely grave if I do; I will therefore end my labours at ten o'clock each night and make up the time lost by labouring on the Sunday.[53]

A man appearing in a Hammersmith court in 1869 made a similar complaint, saying that he could not maintain his family if he only worked six days a week.[54] In making Saturday a half-day holiday, the Factory Act did something to give extra time for rest; but it was not a measure which brought the workers to church in great numbers by relieving the pressure on their one free day. The pattern of spending all or part of Sunday in bed or asleep was a tradition that died hard among labouring men. At the end of the century, the vicar of a country town in the south of England wrote of the apathy of his parishioners regarding Sunday observance: 'I am afraid I have many working men in my parish who have not even Sunday clothes, and who pay no observance to Sunday, except to stay in bed in the morning and eat more than they do on any other days, and have better food. It is indifference, not hostility to religion.'[55] At the same time, Booth observed that in London the bell which summoned the middle class to morning service awakened the working man and his family at eleven o'clock[56] or later; they took their time over lunch[57] and sat half dressed at breakfast as the churchgoers went by.[58]

There are other forms of rejection that are equally mild. In 1902 Booth noted that 'beards will grow after 12 o'clock on Saturday night and the working classes continue to find Sunday a convenient

D

time for being shaved'.[59] Or again, in the words of the poet Louis MacNeice, 'Man's heart expands to tinker with his car.'[60] But the rejection of the bourgeois Sunday has not always taken the form of an indifference to it or a reluctant departure from accepted ways. Marx estimates at 200,000 the crowd which for three hours of that June Sunday afternoon in 1855 menaced and abused those who passed by them in carriages in Oxford Market.[61]

Nor has the violent opposition been restricted to secular parties. Sectarian religion, addressing itself to dispossessed minorities and characterized by an overt rejection of worldly values,[62] has established norms relating to the use of Sunday radically different from those of the church-type and denomination-type of religious institution of the middle class. A barrister of the Established Church, George Chambers, took great exception to the sounding of trumpets on a Sunday morning by the Salvation Army of his town, Eastbourne; this he regarded as 'a desecration of the Sabbath'. Eastbourne protected itself against such distasteful activities by securing an Act of Parliament, the Eastbourne Improvement Act of 1885, which preserved a quiet observance in the town until the act was repealed in the House of Commons in 1892 by 269 votes to 122; the residents of Eastbourne, however, voted 470 in favour of the repeal and 3,257 against it. It was this weight of conservative opinion that earlier had immediately extinguished a band that began to play outside Eastbourne's Burlington Hotel. Recording these events in 1910, Chambers expressed his 'deliberate conviction that the desecration of Sunday which has now reached such alarming proportions, lies in no insignificant degree at the door of "General" Booth with his Sunday bands, Sunday journeyings and Sunday hawking of newspapers'.[63] A parish priest in Portsmouth who could not hear himself preach for the noise in the street, on hearing that the Salvation Army intended to purchase a Baptist hall in his parish went to the auction himself and outbid them in order to keep the nuisance at bay.[64]

Throughout the 1880s there were persistent conflicts between the Salvation Army and its provocateurs. The Sheffield Riot of 1882 was one of several incidents in the country which resulted in military assistance being enlisted and the Riot Act being read.[65] A battle at Worthing in 1884 started on Sunday morning and raged until the Wednesday evening, when the 4th (Royal Irish) Dragoon Guards arrived from Brighton. The local press could not uphold the Salvation Army in this affair: 'The reason for all this was the ill-advised determination of the Salvation Army to parade the streets on Sunday last with the usual noisy accompaniments to their marches, in face of the fact that there was known to exist in the town a very strong feeling against what is looked upon by almost all as a great nuisance.'[66] However, the press expresses the attitude of the respectable people of a residential town and it is important to notice that those arrested as troublemakers could not be so described; the only occupation given is 'fish hawker'[67] but we may gather from their obscene language and their use of shovels in the affray that they were not men of the calibre of George Chambers.

A set of 'Rules for Open-air work' was drawn up by General Booth to advise his soldiers how to handle the police.[68] He announced that in 1884 over 500 Salvationists went to prison for their activities.[69] In giving judgment on an appeal in the Court of the Queen's Bench, Mr Justice Cave described another such incident that had occurred at Weston-super-Mare as 'a very sad state of things to take place on a Sunday in an English town'.[70] In so abusing the English Sunday, General Booth's mission had waged war on a sacred institution of the respectable middle class.

It has been generally true that official restrictions on Sunday activities have been the more happily accepted by the middle class; the working-class pattern of life can only accommodate a Sabbath with difficulty. For the man who works five and a half days a week, Sunday is reserved for leisure and leisure for Sunday. Dominant middle-class groups have determined public life in a way that has suited their own patterns of behaviour but has inhibited and oppressed those without private facilities and a disposition that is other than public.

It does not follow that the Sabbath has been deliberately used by the middle classes as an area in which they may exercise social control. Rather has it been the case that they found in the fourth commandment an acceptable authority for universalizing the kind of observance that their own circumstances afforded, and did not appreciate at first that such an enforced observance would bring hardship to the masses. The stereotype that evolved identified the powerful conservative group with the middle class and the vociferous radicals with the workers. Such an analysis is facile and misleading. For there were working people who accepted and adapted themselves to sabbatarian rigours, just as those who decried a strict observance were often of the educated and prosperous sectors of society. 'Working-class oppression' was less a description of the process by which Sunday observance was enforced or the expression of a personally-felt grievance, than the political slogan of liberal and humanitarian groups within the middle class.

Nevertheless, it is important to remember that it was as an inter-class conflict that the issue was understood by those who took part, and there was much to support such a view in the glimpses of working-class life available to the liberal campaigners. In fact, the relaxation of Sunday observance has not been purely a conflict between the working and middle classes, and the person who shouted at the secretary of the Lord's Day Observance Society 'You're not a working man' need not have been a working man himself.

NOTES

1. J. R. Vincent, *Formation of the Liberal Party 1857–1868*, Constable 1966, p. 79.

2. Karl Marx and Friedrich Engels, *On Religion*, Foreign Languages Publishing House, Moscow 1955, p. 130 (essay written by Marx in London, 25 June 1855).

3. Brian Harrison, 'The Sunday Trading Riots of 1855', *The Historical Journal* vol. viii, 1965, p. 228.

4. Harrison, 'Sunday Trading Riots', p. 225.

5. G. Rude, 'The Study of Popular Disturbances in the "Pre-Industrial Age" ' *Historical Studies*, Melbourne 1963, vol. x.

6. *The Times* Editorial, 15 June 1855, p. 7.

7. Brian Harrison, 'Religion and Recreation in Nineteenth Century England' *Past and Present*, 38, 1967, p. 103.

8. Harrison, 'Religion and Recreation', p. 105.

9. S. Maccoby, *English Radicalism 1886–1914*, Allen and Unwin 1953, pp. 481–82.

10. Harrison, Religion and Recreation, p. 110.

11. Ibid., p. 112.

12. W. J. Reader, *Life in Victorian England*, Batsford 1964, p. 137.

13. K. S. Inglis, *Churches and the Working Classes in Victorian England*, Routledge and Kegan Paul 1963, p. 76.

14. Wilhelm Thomas, 'Sabbatarianism', *Encyclopedia of the Lutheran Church* ed. Julius Bodensieck, Augsberg Publishing House, Minneapolis, 1965, vol. iii, p. 2090.

15. A Layman of the Church of England, *Observations on the Employment of Carriages etc. to and from places of public worship on the Lord's Day*, London 1840.

George Holden, *The Christian Sabbath; or an Inquiry into the Religious Obligation of Keeping Holy one day in seven*, London 1825.

Frederic Peake, *Has Sunday Opening of Museums, Art Galleries and Libraries, been a success? A question for the governing bodies of such institutions*, Lord's Day Observance Society, London 1908.

16. AntiJudaeus (pseud.), *The Sunday not the Jewish Sabbath; a letter to the late Sir Andrew Agnew, Baronet, Together with Calvin on the Jewish Sabbath, or Seventh Day of the Week*, London 1850.

Anonymous, *Sabbaths, an Inquiry into the Origin of Septenary Institutions and the Authority for a Sabbatical Observance of the Modern Sunday* London 1850.

H. Snell, *The Case for Sunday Games, against Sabbatarian Prejudice*, London 1923.

17. Harrison, 'Religion and Recreation', p. 109.

18. Charles Booth, *Life and Labour of the People of London*, Macmillian 1902, Final volume, pp. 47–48.

19. Ibid., p. 48.

20. Harrison, 'Religion and Recreation', p. 104.

21. G. M. Trevelyan, *English Social History*, Longmans Green 1944, p. 493.

22. David Jenkins, Emrys Jones, T. Jones Hughes and Trefor M. Owen, *Welsh Rural Communities* ed. Elwyn Davies and Alwyn D. Rees, University of Wales Press, Cardiff 1960, p. 107.

23. F. G. Roe, *The Victorian Child*, Phoenix House 1959, p. 55.

William Wilberforce, *A Practical View of the prevailing religious system of Professed Christians, in the higher and middle classes of this country, contrasted with real Christianity*, London 1805, p. 207 (first published 1797).

24. E. T. Davies, *Religion in the Industrial Revolution in South Wales*, University of Wales Press, Cardiff 1965, p. 64, (the 1962 Pantfedwyn Lectures).

C. R. Williams, 'The Welsh Religious Revival 1904–5', *The British Journal of Sociology*, iii, 1952, p. 251.

25. M. G. Glazebrook, 'Sunday', *Encyclopedia of Religion and Ethics*, ed. James Hastings, vol. xii, T. and T. Clark 1921, p. 109.

26. R. C. K. Ensor, *England 1870–1914*, Clarendon Press 1960, p. 309.

27. Booth, op. cit., p. 49.

28. Glazebrook, op. cit., p. 110.

29. Alan Smith, 100 *Facts you should know about the Christian Sabbath or the Lord's Day*, Lord's Day Observance Society, currently available, p. 9.

30. Harrison, 'Sunday Trading Riots', p. 220.

31. *Brighton Gazette and Lewes Observer*, 6 February 1840, p. 2.

32. F. Engels, *Condition of the Working Class in England*, Basil Blackwell 1958, p. 319.

33. H. Snell, op. cit., passim.

34. Marx and Engels, op. cit., p. 128.

35. D. Caradog Jones (ed.), *The Social Survey of Merseyside*, Hodder and Stoughton 1934, vol. ii, p. 208.

36. Robert R. Dolling, *Ten years in a Portsmouth slum*, London, 3rd ed. 1897, pp. 131–32.

37. Booth, op. cit., p. 47.

38. Harrison, 'Sunday Trading Riots', p. 222.

39. Marx and Engels, op. cit., p. 129.

40. Ensor, op. cit., pp. 309–10.

41. W. B. Trevelyan, *Sunday*, Longmans Green 1902, p. 97.

42. Maccoby, op. cit., pp. 482–83.

43. Booth, op. cit., pp. 51–52.

M. Marples, *A History of Football*, Secker & Warburg 1954, p. 167.

44. Ensor, op. cit., p. 140.

45. A Layman of the Church of England, op. cit., p. 7.

46. H. Hamilton Maughan, *Some Brighton Churches*, Faith Press 1922, p. 7.

47. H. E. Bracey, *English Rural Life; Village Activities, Organizations and Institutions*, Routledge and Kegan Paul 1959, p. 136.
48. Marx and Engels, op. cit., pp. 129–30.
49. E. T Davies, op. cit., p. 19.
50. *The Times*, 'Amateur Sports on Sunday; Archbishop of York and Right to Recreation', 2 July 1947, p. 7, col. 6.
51. R. Mudie Smith, *The Religious Life of London*, Hodder and Stoughton 1904, p. 20 (quoting Percy Alden, *The Problem of East London*).
52. British Parliamentary Papers, *Industrial Revolution: Children's Employment* ed. P. Ford, Irish University Press, Shannon 1968, vol. vi, pp. 106 and 123.
53. F. Engels, *Condition of the Working Class in England*, p. 215 (reproducing a letter that appeared in the *Morning Chronicle*, 9 December 1843, p. 3, col. 4).
54. Harrison, 'Religion and Recreation', p. 110.
55. W. B. Trevelyan, op. cit., pp. 101–02.
56. Booth, op. cit., pp. 47–48
57. W. J. Reader, op. cit., p. 111.
58. Booth, op. cit., p. 47.
59. Booth, vol. iv, p. 276.
60. Louis MacNeice, 'Sunday Morning'.
61. Marx and Engels, op. cit., p. 130.
62. David Martin, *A Sociology of English Religion*, Heinemann and SCM Press 1967, pp. 79–80.
63. George F. Chambers, *East Bourne Memories of the Victorian Period 1845–1901 and some other things of interest divers and sundry*, V. T. Sumfield, Eastbourne 1910, p. 210.
64. Dolling, op. cit., p. 27.
65. Robert Sandall, *The History of the Salvation Army*, Nelson 1950, vol. ii, pp. 176–77.
66. *Sussex Express*, 23 August 1884, p. 3, col. 2.
67. Ibid., p. 3, col. 3.
68. Sandall, op. cit., p. 311.
69. Ibid., p. 192.
70. Ibid., p. 329.

7 Superstition and Religion: the God of the Gaps

Nicholas Abercrombie, John Baker,
Sebastian Brett and Jane Foster

Introduction

Whatever we are, we are *not* a secular society, particularly if by that omnibus adjective we mean an increasing approximation of average thinking to the norms of natural and social science. . . . There is a luxuriant theological undergrowth which provides the working core of belief more often than is realized . . . our society remains deeply imbued with every type of superstition and metaphysic.[1]

Religious *thinking* is perhaps the area which evidences most conspicuous change. Men act less and less in response to religious motivation: they assess the world in empirical and rational terms, and find themselves involved in rational organizations and rationally determined roles which allow small scope for such religious predilections as they may privately entertain.[2]

There is a chasm between these two positions, one that is partly the use of words, but is primarily a question of fact. The two authors agree on the decline of institutional religion; the dispute is about 'informal' and 'unofficial' metaphysical beliefs – the beliefs that do not form part of the creed of any conventional and acknowledged religion, but which are clearly not scientific or secular. Such beliefs are commonly called superstitions, and it is towards an examination of these beliefs that this article is directed.

The research on which it is based was planned and carried out in spring/summer 1968 by students of the London School of Economics doing an M.Sc. course in sociology or demography. All the

We are particularly indebted to our teachers John Westergaard and Wyn Lewis for initiating and organizing the survey, encouraging us to write this report, and giving us helpful comments on earlier drafts. We must also record our debt to our fellow students without whose hard work in planning and interviewing this article could not have been written. None of these people is responsible for the views expressed in this report.

interviewing was carried out by 19 graduate students with help from 12 undergraduates. The survey was intended mainly as a training exercise in survey method which accounts for its limited scope and for the emphasis on formulating and trying out an interview schedule. However, it was also intended as a pilot investigation into the nature of superstitious beliefs. Because of lack of resources, chiefly time, it was decided that the sample would have to be small and restricted to London. Given these limitations we tried to select a sample in such a way as to provide the most usable set of data. We were particularly interested in the differences between social classes; it was therefore important to select a sample from an area displaying a fairly heterogeneous class composition so that we would be likely to include a sufficiently large number of middle-class people to make comparison possible. Partly for these reasons, and partly for convenience, we chose three neighbouring areas in Islington which, according to the 1966 10% sample census, seemed likely to provide us with a fairly mixed sample.

At the analysis stage, the final group which provided the data for this report numbered 181 persons, all people born outside England and Wales having been excluded. This was 48% of the original sample. (Our 'true' response rate was 64%) Throughout, our analysis has been hampered by the fact that this number is small and some of our more involved points are based on cross-tabulations of very small numbers; this should always be borne in mind. Finally, there are some discrepancies between the age and class distributions of our sample compared with the national distributions on the one hand, and the London distributions on the other. The 30–39 age group is slightly under-represented and the 40–49 group is slightly over-represented, but otherwise the age distributions are similar to the London and national samples. We divided respondents up into nine occupational categories condensed from the socio-economic classification of the 1961 census. On this breakdown our sample does not compare so well with the census data. Professional people are over-represented at the expense of employers and managers, none of whom were included in our sample. Categories 3 and 4 (intermediate and junior non-manual, foremen and skilled manual) are also over-represented while the semi-skilled and the unskilled are under-represented. Because the sample was so small we decided, for the purposes of analysis, to condense the nine occupational groups into two: manual and non-manual. All married women, whether employed or not, were classified according to the occupation of their husbands. Manual was defined so as to include skilled, semi-skilled and unskilled workers, personal service and the armed forces. Non-manual covered the rest, apart from those who were unclassifiable. Unfortunately 10% of our sample fell into this last category, 58% were manual while 32% were non-manual. The comparable figures for Greater London are 60% and 40% and for Islington 72% and 28%. Whether or not our sample actually over-represented the manual or the non-manual depends entirely on the characteristics of those coded 'unclassifiable'.

The prevalence and distribution of superstition

Several writers suggest that modern, industrial societies are 'mentally' closer to primitive societies than might be imagined. For example, Marmor writes: 'As man's scientific knowledge has increased, it is often naturally assumed that irrational beliefs must be diminishing proportionately. Much of our supposed superiority in this regard, however, over earlier or more primitive societies is actually more apparent than real.'[3] Garwood also indicates an alleged lack of symmetry between an advanced 'material development' and the 'amount of superstitious belief and behaviour'.[4]

Our purpose in undertaking this pilot survey was to investigate a set of beliefs that might loosely be described as superstitions. However, lumping together such beliefs (and their associated institutions) into a 'superstitious' or 'magical' category tends to obscure important differences; there is a counter-superstitious ideology as well as a counter-religious one. The classification employed here is one of convenience for we have no theory to guide us in the construction of a rigorous categorization. However, we make a few points here to try to indicate the complexities of these 'styles of thought'.

It is possible to differentiate theoretically between superstitions either on the basis of the type of belief attributed to the individual or in terms of the functions they may serve for individuals or for the social group. These two types of classification are not mutually exclusive; they merely indicate different directions from which the subject may be approached.

When classifying superstitions by belief two dimensions or themes can be distinguished. Firstly, beliefs vary according to the extent to which an outside agency is thought to bring about the expected results of an action or event. Some people's world is inhabited by spirits who cause, for example, bad luck to follow walking under a ladder while others do not connect any agency with their superstitious beliefs. Agency can be ascribed to practically any sort of belief, from lucky numbers, through astrology, to quasi-moral beliefs, such that evil-doers get their deserts. A tendency in societies towards depersonalizing certain features of their environment may perhaps be considered a version of a process of secularization.

The second dimension is the 'scientific' nature of the belief; some superstitious beliefs are in a sense more 'scientific' than others. We mean by this that they employ a pseudo-scientific jargon, they are associated with an almost professional body of practitioners and magazines or, perhaps, the beliefs are taken seriously enough by certain members of the community to warrant a scientific investigation. In this sense, common superstitions like lucky numbers and touching wood are at one end of the 'scientific' continuum, astrology is in the middle, followed by beliefs in ghosts, with telepathy and water divination at the other end. An important point here is that people may be genuinely confused about the likelihood of claims made for the more 'scientific' beliefs and perhaps the more exposed they are to a truly scientific methodology the more likely they are to subscribe to superstitious beliefs which rest on an alleged application of that methodology. Our results have some bearing on this point.

Any study of superstition inevitably runs the risk of over-intellectualizing the beliefs concerned. Not all superstitious observances have the same significance for all people, nor for the same person at at different times. Furthermore, one does not want to construct ponderous theories about the 'function' of practices that are just habitual. Accordingly, we tried to distinguish, amongst those performing any particular superstitious practice, between those who did it 'just from habit' and the rest. It will be seen that we describe only the latter as 'genuine believers' and our explanations are concerned principally with them. However, even if it is correct to describe a particular action as 'just habitual' explanation should not end there. It is still of interest to ask why these particular practices have become habitual. It can be argued that the habitual performance of superstitions such as touching wood stands to a genuine belief in the efficacy of this practice as going to church only for a marriage stands to genuine religious belief. Comparing the frequent participation in the rites of passage to the infrequent attendance at weekly church services MacIntyre says: 'There is such a high figure for participation in these rites, both by the whole population and by the working-class that some further explanation is needed.'[5] Hoggart is also concerned with the importance of the habitual: 'They say "Oh, it's all superstition", and look at popular magazine articles which discount them, but still they pick them up verbally and pass them on and this applies to young people as much as to the old.'[6]

[It is regrettable that it was not possible to test the coherence of sets of beliefs within individuals, i.e. whether one can talk of superstitions as forming a style of thought. Unfortunately our questionaire did not lend itself immediately to a Guttman scaling or similar technique.]

In discussion of the 'function' of superstitious behaviour, writers frequently refer to various versions of what one might call the theory of adjustment to the uncertain environment. It is important to realize that there is by no means a single coherent, accepted version and there are various behaviours to be accounted for. For example, there are attempts to manipulate the environment by the use of lucky charms; there are attempts to evade bad luck as in touching wood; there are portents or predictions such as black cats or astrology, some of which may be used to alter planned actions, and some not (those Roman entrails). Finally some superstitious ideas help people to resign themselves to the difficult or unlucky, for example, the idea that bad luck comes in threes. We will return to this question of function in some detail in our conclusions.

Though it seems justifiable, on account of the colloquial use of the term, to describe all the non-religious beliefs about which we asked questions as 'superstitious', it is also apparent that there are important differences between them. Broadly we can distinguish four different types of belief, though there is considerable overlap between them. Firstly, we asked questions about specific superstitions such as the significance of black cats, the number 13 and walking under ladders. Secondly, we asked a number of questions about beliefs in quasi-scientific subjects such as astrology, premonitions and ghosts. Thirdly, we tried to investigate the belief in fate as a potentially harmful force which must be cajoled, placated and certainly not tempted. This type of belief has strong moral overtones and rests, at least in part, on something akin to the Greek concept of *hubris*. Moral attitudes are again implicated in the fourth group of questions, those concerned with particular world-views such as the belief that luck is necessary for happiness or success or that the world is a fair place.

To accept, even in part, any of these four sorts of beliefs would probably be described colloquially as 'superstitious'. Thus the answers to the question: 'Are you on the whole superstitious?' probably reflected the respondents' own estimate of their attitude to all these subjects. One-third of our sample declared themselves to be superstitious, though many of these people had reservations. One elderly woman remarked significantly that she was superstitious, but 'only on the good things, not the bad'. There was no difference between the social classes, though considerably more men than women answered 'No'.

Turning to the specific superstitious practices, there appeared to be wide variations in their popularity. Over three-quarters of the sample touched wood in certain situations and almost half of them threw salt over their shoulders if some was spilled. There is then a big jump to the belief in lucky numbers (22%), and charms (18%), the evasion of ladders, and the belief that black cats bring good luck (both 15%). Only one in ten people thought the number 13 was unlucky.

How should one evaluate these figures? As already suggested, though the action may be performed it may have very little significance for the individual concerned. We tried to discover more about the beliefs behind the practices by asking people whether or not they became uneasy if, for some reason, they did not perform the right action in the appropriate circumstances. Here it seems that the less common superstitious practices are more actively supported by those performing the actions. Nearly all those who thought the number 13 unlucky said they would feel uneasy if they lived in a house numbered 13. Just under half of those who tried to avoid ladders (for non-secular reasons) said they felt uneasy if they failed to do so, whereas only 8% of the host of wood-touchers (77%) expressed a similar attitude. This fraction of 'uneasy people' remained fairly constant through several questions (it varied between 6% and 8%).

On the same principle of trying to get at the beliefs behind these actions, we asked in what sort of situations people touched wood. Forty per cent of our sample gave specific answers (a significantly high figure) and thus, although few were anxious, a large minority could give some account of their beliefs. Traditionally, the superstition is meant to provide insurance against harm to some hoped for event in the future. Most people did come roughly into this category, in that they touched wood to avoid future harm, but the overtones of tempting fate were frequently missing ('I have got a bad leg and when it begins to get bad, I touch wood in order that it doesn't get worse'). Other intentions were mentioned, such as the relief of a present difficulty or the simple fulfilment of a wish, as in the comment 'If I want something to happen very much, I say touch wood and whistle.' A significant aspect of answers to this question was the large number of specific references to health, especially among women, a point also noted by Hoggart.

For the 'superstitious' questions in this section one of the most strongly marked features was the difference between the number of superstitious responses of men and women. This finding is common to all surveys. Given the direction there was some variability as to strength, from 18% differences for salt-throwing and possession of a charm, to 7% for walking under a ladder, to a 1% difference for touching wood. For questions relating to unease felt when not performing the appropriate superstitious action, the sex differences were still present. However, the absolute numbers were rather small, so one cannot form a firm judgment. Apart from touching wood, the one exception to the generalization of clear differences between men and women was in the question of lucky numbers, where there was no difference at all. One suggestion is that since men gamble much more than women, they may be much keener on devices which bring them luck in this activity.

The evidence about class and age is more various and inconclusive. Class differences were virtually nil. There was a slight tendency for manual workers to be more superstitious than non-manual in walking under ladders and number 13, but it was not statistically significant. There was a larger (6%) difference in the same direction for salt-throwing but for touching wood there was a 5% difference in the opposite direction. It seems that the practice of touching wood is unlike all the other superstitions considered. It is much more widely followed in daily behaviour and is equally popular amongst both men and women.

With age, there were one or two important consistencies. The oldest age-group (over 60) was usually the most superstitious (the only exception again being touching wood), followed by the youngest. The least superstitious was the 50–59-year-old group. Part but not all of the age differences are due to the sex composition of the age-groups; for example the two most superstitious groups (20–29 and over 60) both have a preponderance of women (55% women to 45% men and 68% women to 32% men respectively). However, there is a residual age-effect. To use a crude index, the 40–49 age group is almost as superstitious as the 20–29 age group but has the highest proportion of men of any of the groups (58% men to 48% women).

There is one last point concerning this section. Clearly some superstitious rituals are more easily and economically performed than others. This should be taken into account when assessing our results and might perhaps influence the distributions on various questions. The ease of touching wood may account for the low sex differences on the question; it may be an observance without great meaning.

The answers to our second group of questions, those dealing with astrology, ghosts and premonitions, reflect the fact that there is much more debate about the realities of claims in these subjects. Furthermore, associated with astrology or spiritualism is a body of techniques, groups of devout practitioners and large numbers of journals. Because of the quasi-scientific aura of these subjects people are evidently much more uncertain about them than they are about the various superstitious beliefs already discussed. For example, 12% of our respondents did not know whether they believed in ghosts or spirits and a similar proportion were not sure whether the movement of stars or planets affected events on earth. Twenty-eight per cent were not sure whether there was a life after death. ('Don't know' answers to the questions about common superstitious beliefs rarely rose above 3%.) Puzzlement was expressed in some comments, as if the matters being discussed needed a great deal more research or the knowledge was available but the respondent was unable to get at it. One young man who was clearly very sceptical about astrology nevertheless did not want to damn it completely because 'I've never read a book on it but there could be something in it.'

Some 60% of our sample said they looked at horoscopes, and a third did so regularly. The reasons given for *not* looking at them were often rather idiosyncratic; one man in his sixties said: 'I don't look because I'm frightened.' Formal knowledge of astrology is even better rooted in the population, since some 80% knew which sign of the zodiac they were born under.

It may be argued that people do not really believe in horoscopes but only read them for fun. This is not quite an analogous argument with that discussed above concerning habit and 'real belief', but it is similar. In any event, as will be shown, those who 'really believe' in aspects of astrology are a much larger group (9–23%) than those who 'really believe' in the efficacy of superstitions (6–8%). Thus when asked 'What would you say are the main things that you get out of reading the stars?', 15% said that they acted as a guide (one man in his twenties simply said 'the truth'), and a further 9% gave reasons mixing this sort of answer with, for example, curiosity, like the young woman who answered 'For a bit of fun and hope'. These two kinds of reasons combined give an 'astrological' group of 23%. Thirty per cent gave reasons which disclaimed any astrological belief; these ranged from 'curiosity' to 'habit' to 'get a laugh'. It is clear that the group giving answers tied in some way to belief in astrology is large enough to make a detailed examination worth while.

The most obvious purpose of the horoscopes is to foretell the future. As expected, most of the people who appeared to believe in the stars said this was why they read them, and 9% said they took account of what the stars said in their everyday life. Similarly, when asked why they thought a particular column was good or bad the criterion most frequently mentioned by both believers and non-believers was the accuracy of its forecasts. However, there obviously are other, possibly unconscious, benefits to be derived from reading the stars. For example, nearly one-third of the people who read them (17% of the total) thought that the stars helped them 'to understand what kind of person they were' and a similar number believed that the stars could say whether two people were likely to get on together, particularly in marriage. Again, there is evidence to suggest that reading the columns helps to relieve anxiety, possibly even in the minds of those who don't really believe in them. It is very noticeable that the stars columns in the newspapers and magazines all tend to be optimistic most of the time. Moreover it seems that people take more notice of the stars if they forecast something pleasant. Nearly one-third of all those who read the columns at all said they were 'given encouragement by the stars when things were going badly'. One woman summed it up: 'On odd occasions when things are in a bad way it helps – a sort of straw to cling on to.'

Some 60% of our respondents believed in premonitions and 38% had had one that turned out to be true. Thirty per cent believed that there were 'ghosts or spirits that can sometimes be seen or sensed by people', and 15% had come across something of this kind. However, only 18% of the sample had visited a palmist, fortune teller or astrologist; we felt that this was improbably low, especially when compared with Gorer's figure of 44%.

There were the expected differences between men and women in answers to astrological questions. They are, however, much larger than those for the previous sections; for the question 'Do you look at horoscopes?' the difference is 25%. However, for the questions on ghosts and premonitions the difference is a good deal smaller and for those who have actually had experiences of ghosts or premonitions the difference has disappeared entirely. There were no class or age differences for these two questions but the lower class were consistently more astrologically inclined than the upper class, and for some questions the difference was striking. The age-distributions were in most cases very similar to those obtained by the first group of superstition questions; the youngest and the oldest were the most superstitious and the 30–39 and 50–59 age groups were the least.

These differences between the findings about astrology and those about ghosts and premonitions lend support to the view that it is helpful and significant to differentiate between metaphysical beliefs according to their scientific standing. In general, it seems that women and working-class people are most likely to accept these ideas. However, assuming that men and middle-class people are less confident of their scepticism in the case of beliefs having an aura of scientific respectability one would expect these differentials to be least pronounced in the case of the most 'scientific' beliefs. One can argue that astrology is a subject of considerably less scientific respectability than ghosts, premonitions and telepathy – witness the number of serious articles on these subjects in reputable scientific journals. This argument can therefore help to explain the fact that we found greater differences between the sexes and the classes in answers to the questions about astrology than on the questions about ghosts and premonitions. It is interesting that the Opinion Research Centre asking a wider range of questions than we did, found sex differences for fortune-telling but not for telepathy or faith-healing. Similarly the middle class was more sceptical than the working class about astrological fortune-telling but not about faith-healing and communication with the dead.[9]

We asked two questions designed to discover whether people

believed in 'fate' as a powerful force in their lives: 'If you seemed to be having a period of good luck would you be worried by a feeling that this was likely to turn into bad luck?' and '. . . would you make a point of not talking too much about it, in order not to tempt fate?' Although in answer to the first question only 18% confessed to conscious anxiety, a quarter said they would avoid talking about their good luck. Men and manual workers were slightly more prone to this sort of anxiety than women and middle-class people. Any conclusions from such slender evidence must be tentative but it does seem possible that the fear of fate and the feeling of *hubris*, integral both to these ideas and to the practice of touching wood, are more 'masculine' than the common superstitious beliefs discussed earlier. An American psychologist, discussing the practice of touching wood explains it as a symbolic gesture serving as an outlet for aggressive emotions. 'The competitive nature of our social structure makes every person a potential rival for the goods and gratifications of life. One of the common techniques employed for warding off the envy and hostility inherent in such rivalry is to deny or minimize one's own prosperity or good fortune.'[10] This type of explanation for the apparent 'fear of fate' is perhaps more appropriate than one which sees it as an element of supernatural belief.

The last group of questions is concerned above all with the ideas of luck and fairness. Unfortunately the interpretation of replies is made very difficult by the vagueness of these concepts. In many uses the word 'luck' can have either metaphysical or secular connotations. The more articulate or loquacious respondents explained what they meant but many did not. But despite these difficulties the interest of the subject seems to justify some discussion since beliefs on the boundary between metaphysics and the social world remain comparatively unexplored.

In answer to the question 'Do you think the world is a fair place?' almost half the sample said 'Yes', women being in a slightly higher proportion than men. Perhaps surprisingly, a higher proportion of middle-class people, both men and women, answered 'No'. In some cases the question seems to have been interpreted as referring to social, genetic or environmental benefits. Other people evidently thought it referred to some notion of retributive justice. However, moral codes differ, and with them attitudes towards justice. Two women, both of whom thought the world was unfair, gave opposite reasons for their answers: 'No one really deserves to suffer', and

'Thank God no one gets what they deserve or we should all be a lot worse off.' Another 60-year-old married woman related the concept of fairness closely to her own experiences in life: 'The world is unfair because young people now can live off the state. The world is only fair if you work.'

Two out of three people in both sexes seemed to believe that some people were born lucky and went through life protected against misfortune. Many people were obviously thinking of social advantages such as background or wealth but others clearly saw luck in a much less secular sense: 'It's like having somebody sitting on your shoulders keeping you out of harm's way and telling you what to do.' There does seem to be some relationship between this belief and specific superstitions discussed earlier. Nine out of ten of the people who appeared to be very superstitious on the latter believed that certain people were born lucky while less than half of those giving very unsuperstitious answers to the earlier questions shared this attitude. There was no class difference in male answers to this question but many more working-class women appeared to believe in lucky people than women whose husband's occupations was non-manual. Indeed, middle-class women were more sceptical than men of either class.

Class again seems to have an effect in determining an individual's estimate of the relationship between luck and achievement. When asked 'Which is more important for success, luck or hard work and ability?', one in ten of the respondents picked luck while another 25% considered all three to be of equal importance. One in five working-class men rated luck as more important compared to only one in twenty of the men in non-manual occupations. It is interesting that whereas women were more likely to believe in the various little superstitious practices such as throwing salt men appeared to give more weight to the general importance of luck in their lives. Three times as many men as women thought luck more important for success than hard work or ability. Moreover, this relationship between the sexes is exactly mirrored in the answers to the question 'How important do you think being lucky is for happiness?' 17% of the men answered 'very important'; only 6% of the women did so.

Thus luck seems to be a masculine concept and, amongst men at least, a particularly working-class concept. However, to believe in luck is not necessarily superstitious or non-rational. For the middle-class man 'luck' may be a superstitious apology for failure but for the working-class man it may be a simple empirical judgment. The female insistence on hard work and ability as the important causes of success could also be seen as due to less, rather than more, rationalism on the part of women. 'Success' may still be a particularly masculine concept; in discussing it women may be thinking of their husbands' career more than their own lives. Since, however, they have less first-hand knowledge of the man's work situation they may subscribe less critically to a belief in the prevalence of achievement criteria. The male, especially the working-class male, is perhaps more sceptical about the real determinants of success.

The analysis of religious belief

There is no clear-cut philosophical distinction between 'religious' and 'superstitious' belief. Yet there is normally a firm theological distinction and many of the ideas we investigated were illegitimate from any theological viewpoint. Before discussing the relationship between superstition and religion, we present our findings as to the religious composition of our sample.

Church affiliation was broadly comparable to that described in other studies. Sixty-eight per cent of our respondents described themselves as Church of England, 9% as Roman Catholic, 9% as belonging to other Christian groups and 4% as belonging to non-Christian religions; 9% denied having a religion.

Roughly similar proportions of men and women belonged to the Church of England, but twice as many women as men said they were Roman Catholic. Twice as many men as women had no religion. For men religious affiliation increased with age though this was not the case with women.

Nominal affiliation, in our sample as elsewhere, bore little relationship to actual belief or practice. Over half never went to a place of worship, 5% went once a month, 2% twice a month and 8% every week or more frequently. Belief in the existence of a God was very high – over three-quarters of the total (87% of women and 63% of men). But the reasons for belief vary: 'It's a duty to perform; none of us would be around if it weren't for him', said one man to whom religion was 'very unimportant'. Another who gave totally non-religious answers to all the other questions said about belief in God: 'Well, it would be wicked to say I don't believe. I sat on a jury once and swore by God. I should have said then if I didn't believe.' Two other people, a man and a woman, simply said in answer to this question: 'You have to, don't you?' Others seemed to feel the need for the existence of some sort of omnipotent being – 'something more powerful than us' – as one woman put it. Another totally non-religious young married woman took the same line: 'I think there is someone somewhere who must have put us here.' For some the magnificent complexity of the universe produces the opposite effect. One woman who said she had believed in God until three years ago explained: 'What changed it was going to the Planetarium. I took my child. I never saw the world again as I saw it before. No one could possibly rule. I never thought the world was so large. But I continued to send my kids to Sunday School. . . . I wanted them to know religion goes on.'

Trying to pin down a more genuinely religious belief in God we asked respondents: 'Do you believe in a God who can change the course of events on earth?' Unfortunately, a considerable number of people seem to have had difficulty understanding this question. One married woman answered, 'No, just the ordinary one', and another older woman clearly considered the question superfluous: 'I just believe in God Almighty and that's all there is to it.' However, the number who actually answered 'don't know' is quite small – 8% of the total. Almost exactly half of those who believed in God (36% of the total) saw him as an interventionist being.

A surprisingly large proportion of people said that religion was 'very important' to them – 20% of women and 15% of men. If we add to this group those who answered 'fairly important' the total for whom religion had some importance is 33% (40% of women and 26% of men). These figures were more or less repeated in the answers to the question about private prayer; 37% of the total (47% of women and 24% of men) said they prayed in private 'often' and a further 22% prayed sometimes.

It may well be that the majority of those who pray 'sometimes' do so only in moments of great stress – when they are extremely frightened, worried or unhappy. They perhaps say a little prayer as a last resort when all else has failed and to provide comfort. For example, one elderly unmarried woman who did not believe in God said that she did pray quite often 'for a little bit of comfort'. Another man who appeared non-religious on most questions said he did not usually pray 'but if there is someone you love in trouble you say, "please help him".' Similarly, quite a few people said they had prayed during the war although not at other times.

There was a relatively high belief in the *efficacy* of prayer. Forty-five per cent of the total (60% of women, 30% of men) believed their prayers were sometimes answered. A few people said that they did not pray for favours and others didn't believe that their prayers were ever answered. 'The important thing is that you feel better in yourself', said one woman. The comparison of figures for prayer and for church attendance support the theory that religion is becoming a private rather than an institutional observance. Moreover, being a Christian is evidently now seen much more as a matter of accepting and practising a certain moral code rather than as active membership of a church. One man who was born a Roman Catholic but no longer practised any religion commented: 'Probably there are more religious people now than there ever were before but they don't go to church. People now are better Christians generally.' The idea, 'you don't have to go to church to be good' was specifically mentioned several times and implied by many more answers. Many people said they had turned away from religion because it was 'rammed down their throats when they were young'. Despite this, many apparently non-religious people said they gave their children religious instruction and sent them to Sunday School. 'I believe it's an anchor in life', one agnostic father explained. 'I'm teaching it to the kid so he'll have an anchor though I don't believe in any of it.' It is presumably only in this sense of 'Christian' that it is possible to say that 'the vast majority of English people identify themselves with the word "Christian".' However, our exploration of the interconnections between self-professed religiosity, church attendance and superstitiousness, discussed below, made us wonder just what it means to call such people *religious*.

All the figures concerned with religious belief and practice tend to suggest that roughly one-third of the respondents held quite genuine religious beliefs and regarded religion as of some importance in their lives although many fewer actually went to church. All the questions, except that asking for simple religious affiliation, provide evidence of the expected difference between male and female respondents, the men being consistently less religious and more sceptical than the women. The difference is biggest of all on the question referring to formal religious observance – nearly three times as many women as men went to church once a month or more often. Just under twice as many women prayed in private. However, of those who did pray, roughly the same percentage of men and women believed that their

prayers were sometimes answered (three-quarters in each case). Of
those who did pray, the percentage of women who did not believe
that their prayers were answered was twice the similar percentage of
men, whereas a higher proportion of men said they either didn't
know or didn't pray for favours.

The difference is slightly less striking in the other religious questions dealing with pure beliefs. Eighty-seven per cent of the women
believed in a God, compared to only 63% of the men, whereas four
times as many men were prepared to say categorically that they did
not believe. Of those who did believe in a God, about the same proportion of men and women saw him as an interventionist being (42%
of male believers and 47% of female believers).

It is well known that women are more religious than men. However, a secondary reason for the difference between the sexes may be
that women are more susceptible to the social pressures that encourage religious answers. For some people, particularly at the upper end
of the social scale, religion is a subject endowed with status connotations. Thus there may be a tendency for women, particularly
middle-class women or those aspiring to middle-class status, both
to be more assiduous in their religious observances because this
brings social prestige, and to exaggerate in their answers the extent
of their religious devotion. Our survey provides some evidence in
support of this theory. Middle-class women of every age-group were
more likely to go to church than working-class women. Similarly,
middle-class women were more likely to say that religion was important to them – a question which is particularly loaded with status
connotations. Half the middle-class women said religion was either
very important or fairly important to them as compared to only 35%
of the working-class women. Sixty per cent of middle-class women
prayed in private often while only 43% of working-class women did
so. Again, middle-class women in every age-group appeared more
likely to believe in an after-life than working-class women.

It is interesting to see that class seemed to have almost no effect on
the answers given by men to all these questions. For them age seemed
more important. Unfortunately, since the number of men in the
sample was very small, one cannot place too much reliance on the
figures. However, our figures, such as they are, suggest the following
tendencies. Men tend to pray more often as they get older, although
they have a low point in their thirties and forties. Working-class men
are less likely to go to church as they get older; 80% of those over

60 never went as compared to only a quarter of those in their twenties. Just over a quarter of the men of both classes said that religion had some importance for them. However, it would seem that age had a similar effect on their answers to this question as on the frequency of private prayer. Middle-class men tend to regard religion as of least importance to them when they are in their thirties; it then increases steadily in importance as they get older. In the case of working-class men the pattern is much less regular, although here again the lowest point is in the age group 30–40.

Belief in God seemed to be more common among working-class people, both men and women, as they got older. However, this was not true of middle-class people where the pattern of disbelief appeared to be quite arbitrary. There were no discernible trends with regard to belief in an interventionist God, although it would seem that a higher proportion of working-class people either did not understand the question or answered 'don't know'. One might expect belief in an after-life to vary quite strikingly with age but our figures do not support this. If we divide our religious questions into two groups, religious practices like church attendance, and praying and pure beliefs, we find that, in the case of the former group of questions, class seems to have more effect on women and age more effect on men, whereas in the latter group neither factor seems to be particularly relevant for either sex.

The data we have obtained on religion indicates that our sample was considerably less religious than the sample used by Gorer to compile *Exploring English Character*. It is possible that these figures represent a decline in religious belief and behaviour since Gorer's study was published in 1935. However, it is much more likely that the disparities are due to differences in the composition of the two samples. Our sample was drawn from one particular area of London, whereas Gorer's was drawn from all over England and Wales. Gorer himself found that both religious belief and religious observance were less frequent in the large towns than in the smaller towns and villages and that this was particularly pronounced in the case of London.

Gorer did not specifically ask about belief in God, but a survey carried out by Mass Observation in 1948[12] produced figures very similar to ours. Of particular interest was their finding that a substantial proportion of agnostics (25%) pray, and that many people, when asked the subject of their prayers, answered in terms of their state of mind while praying, rather than the subject itself. Six in ten of the prayers of those who doubted or denied the existence of God were pleas for protection in a time of crisis, as compared to only three in ten of those who said they believed in God. This supports the view, suggested by our evidence, that for many, particularly agnostics, praying represents principally a source of comfort. In this way it may be that prayer satisfies a similar need for some people that astrology does for others.

In the next section we will discuss some preliminary evidence on this and similar questions relating to the connection between superstition and religious belief.

Religion and superstitiousness

On the basis of their answers to a selected number of questions, the respondents were divided into four groups of increasing degrees of superstitiousness. These groups were based on a count of superstitious answers given, combined with a simple weighting procedure. The following table gives an indication of the size of the groups, and the proportion of the sample they represent.

	Group	No.	Proportion of sample percent
A	Very unsuperstitious	67	28
B	Quite unsuperstitious	70	30
C	Quite supersititious	58	24
D	Very superstitious	43	18

A breakdown of the groups suggested that superstitiousness was significantly correlated with both sex and class. Women appeared, as expected, to be more superstitious than men, and manual respondents more than non-manual.

Nearly two-thirds of the least superstitious group were men and over two-thirds of the most superstitious group were women. While the proportion of non-manual respondents in the total sample was under a third, the least superstitious group were almost half non-manual; nearly three-quarters of the most superstitious group were manual.

If we look at the two superstitious groups alone, it is clear that among both women and men, the middle class were less superstitious than the working class However, women were more superstitious than men, regardless of their class. The proportion of working-class women in groups C and D lay above the average for both women as a whole and working-class respondents as a whole. The proportion of middle-class women lay below the average for women, but above the average for all middle-class respondents.

Middle-class men lay at the bottom of the scale, below the average for middle-class respondents and for men; working-class men lay below the average for working-class respondents, but above the average for men. Men were less likely to be in the superstitious groups, regardless of their class: working-class men were on the whole less superstitious than middle-class women. [We would like to emphasize that these findings, which depend on a class/sex breakdown, are not statistically adequate, and hence should be interpreted with great caution. However, we feel that a pilot survey may legitimately be used to supply hypotheses which cannot be wholly supported on its own data.]

Part of our purpose in constructing these groups was to estimate the extent to which the religious minority overlaps with the superstitious minority, and to find out whether atheistic respondents were noticeably less superstitious than believers.

With some reservations, this proved to be the case. About a quarter of our religious respondents were found in the very superstitious group, compared with only 10–14% of the non-religious. A further quarter of the religious respondents were completely unsuperstitious, compared with a third of the non-religious. While religious people were on average distributed evenly between the groups, the non-religious tended to cluster in the unsuperstitious groups. When the superstitious groups were compared on the basis of their answers to the questions on religion, on average, one person in two of the very superstitious gave a religious answer, compared with one in four of the very unsuperstitious.

The relationship between religion and superstition appears to hold for both sex and class groupings. However, women who gave consistently unreligious answers appeared to be more superstitious on average than men who were plainly religious. Similarly, working-class respondents were more superstitious than middle-class, even when the former were unreligious and the latter religious. The probability of middle-class respondents being more or less superstitious than working-class seems to depend, not on the extent of their religiosity, but on their sex. [Again, the reader is asked to bear in mind the very small size of the sub-groups on which these findings are based.]

An example: of the 65 respondents who considered religion to be important in their lives, 52% came from the unsuperstitious groups, while nearly *two-thirds* of those who considered religion to be unimportant came from the unsuperstitious groups. When sex is held constant, the association between religion and superstitiousness is confirmed, for both men and women; however, whether a religious person will be more superstitious than a non-believer seems to depend on his sex. Women who thought religion unimportant were distributed evenly between the superstitious and unsuperstitious groups; men who thought religion important were considerably less superstitious – two-thirds came from the unsuperstitious groups.

Similarly, middle-class respondents tended to be less superstitious than working-class, regardless of the importance they attached to religion. Of the middle-class respondents, under a third of those who considered religion important were superstitious, compared with a quarter of those who attached no importance to religion. Thus there was a slight difference due to religion. Of the working-class respondents, over half of those who attached importance to religion were superstitious, compared to three-eighths of those who thought religion unimportant. Again there was a slight difference due to religion. However, this does not lead us to modify the statement that working-class people are more likely to be superstitious than middle-class people, since the religious middle-class respondents were clearly less likely to fall into the superstitious groups than the working-class disbelievers.

However, an analysis of church attendance suggests that the association between religion and superstitiousness is more complex, and perhaps much more interesting than this. It appears that regular churchgoers were a very special sub-group within the religious minority.

In the first place they were less superstitious than those who never attended church. Of those who went to church regularly every week, 58% were very unsuperstitious, compared with 38% of those who went once a month, and 28% of those who never went. Only 5% of the regular weekly attenders were very superstitious, compared with 16% of those who never darkened a porch. Nearly a quarter of the unsuperstitious went to church at least once a month, while this was true of only one person in twenty of the very superstitious.

This amounts to a dramatic reversal of the expected trend in the relationship between religion and superstition. There is, of course, the possibility that the association is a spurious one due to the correlation between superstition and social class. It is well known that churchgoers are overwhelmingly middle-class, and it is also clear that the middle classes are under-represented in the superstitious groups. Are churchgoers unsuperstitious only because they are middle-class?

Such as it is, the evidence suggests that this is not the case. Of those who said they went to church at least once a month, two-fifths were working-class. The latter were atypically unsuperstitious: only a third of them were in the superstitious groups; if they had been typical of working-class respondents, this proportion should have been nearer a half. What is more, middle-class respondents who said they never went to church were more superstitious than those middle-class people who said they attended regularly. Thus within both classes church attendance was inversely correlated with superstitiousness. The same was true for both men and women. While women as a whole were more superstitious than men, regardless of their devotional loyalty, women who said they never went to church, paradoxically, were as superstitious as those who prayed frequently in private, or believed in life after death. Those who went once a month at least seemed to be *less* superstitious than those who never prayed, or did not believe in a life after death. The effect among men was similar, but less pronounced. However, the relationship was again limited by the overall tendency of women to be more superstitious than men, and by the tendency for the working-class to be more superstitious than the middle-class. Although middle-class non-churchgoers were significantly more superstitious than middle-class churchgoers, they remained slightly less superstitious than working-class people who attended regularly.

The most plausible explanation of the inverse correlation between church attendance and superstitiousness is that the church exercises a genuinely counter-superstitious influence among its adherents. It seems that for many people, probably the great majority, religious beliefs and practices merge almost indistinguishably with superstitions of all sorts, to be summoned only in special situations of crisis and anxiety. Perhaps, amid all this confusion of sentiment, ritual and belief, the church acts, in some way, as a filter, reinforcing the distinction between beliefs which are theologically acceptable, and those which are not, those which have the sanction of divine authority, and those which are 'symptoms of man's prolonged refusal to come of age'. If this is so, we would have to look for an explanation of the relationship between popular superstitions and religious beliefs in the sociological history of the Church of England, in its class origins and associations, and in those social changes which continue to turn the majority away from its doors.

The majority are 'passively religious'. The distinction between beliefs which are backed by ancient scriptures, and those which have come down through word of mouth and are sustained by a way of life is confused in many minds. Has the church for the past two hundred years been the centre of a way of life? Perhaps superstitions are a vestigial expression of community, while the church is an institution in a society of institutions, with a working knowledge of its market and the characteristics of its consumers. It is also an expression of status and mobility, and has certain basic standards of conformity and makes minimum intellectual demands. The clergy actively discriminates between spiritual goods, and in its weekly sermons, provides an on-going comment on the social scene, articulating this in terms of an exclusive set of beliefs which are constantly re-asserted in the light of modern stereotypes.

It may be true that some non-churchgoers prefer to work out their own beliefs, methods of worship and path of salvation. These 'extreme Protestants' present a principled objection to religious authority, taking only what seems to them to be realistic and rational. But the majority probably stay away for other reasons – out of ignorance, apathy, distaste or the sheer competition of other diversions. The point is that religious individualism may be associated with the very reverse of the secular-rational world-view. Apathy may be mistaken for scepticism, ignorance of the claims of religion or dislike of religious pretension. *Puzzled People* emphasized that many of those who were most critical of the church were not the sceptical or the atheistic, not those with an axe to grind, but tolerant well-wishers who resented the priggishness of their neighbours, and whose respect for the church's teaching was only matched by their vagueness as to its content.

Where religion persists among this group, it is passive and little dwelt upon – elbowed into a corner of the mind which it shares with competing beliefs of all kinds, and from where it is summoned at moments in life when habit and know-how cannot assist, and whence it returns in the light of day. The religion of the superstitious seems to be not intense, hardly conscious and only semi-articulate. This would account for the fact that a number of superstitious respondents thought religion only 'fairly important', whereas the majority of the unsuperstitious considered it either 'very important' or 'very unimportant'. Middle-class piety appears to be the other side of the coin of dissident secularity. Unsuperstitious respondents were most likely to be found in two groups: the actively secular and the actively religious. The superstitious respondents were to be found in the confused area between the two.

Evidence of a widespread but only semi-articulate religious sense is provided by the findings we obtained on private prayer. Over a third of the sample said they often prayed in private. This is well over double the number who went to church with any regularity; *over two-thirds* of those who prayed frequently in private rarely if ever went to church. Those who prayed often were often doubtful or uncommitted on questions of belief; a quarter of them did not consider religion to be important in their lives, half did not believe that God could intervene in worldly things. Of those who said they prayed sometimes, nearly two-thirds did not consider religion to be important, three-quarters did not believe in, or were uncertain about an after-life, and over half did not believe that God could intervene. Obviously, those who prayed often showed that religion was rather more relevant to them, but the difference is rather less striking than the similarities between the two groups. In our analysis of the responses we thought it reasonable to treat those who said they prayed often as a religious minority (actually about one in three of the total) equal in size, though not identical in composition to those who think religion 'important' in their lives.

Puzzled People drew a picture of private prayer as 'a great volume of special pleas addressed erratically to the deity, in which the voices of believers and disbelievers mingle in anxiety, fear, and inability to grapple alone; punctuated by long periods of relative quiet when the workaday world presents fewer humanly insoluble problems and humanly insurmountable dangers'.[13] The authors made an explicit analogy with astrology, pointing out that the practice is resorted to when human agency fails or is powerless, but does not imply any *long-standing* belief in, or loyalty towards, the agency invoked. The revival of astrology is, as they put it, 'a symptom suggestive of the meaning and depth of crisis prayer'.

Our findings seem to confirm this thesis. Frequent prayer was significantly related to the respondent's general level of superstitiousness, in both sexes and in both class groupings. It seems reasonable to take an association between prayer and superstitiousness as at least *prima facie* evidence about the nature and function of prayer.

On average, of those who prayed often in private, over half fell into the superstitious groups, while of those who said they never prayed, under a third were superstitious. Over a quarter of the regular prayers were very superstitious, compared with under a tenth of those who never prayed. Over half the very superstitious group said they prayed often, while under one quarter of the totally unsuperstitious said they did so. The difference is most striking among men. While only 20% of the men who never prayed were in the superstitious groups, 40% of those who prayed often were superstitious. However, women proved to be more superstitious regardless of whether they prayed or not, but women who prayed often were more likely to be superstitious than those who never prayed.

If we analyse the distributions of those who prayed often in private, *and* were superstitious, by class, it is evident that those who prayed often tended to have a higher proportion in the superstitious groups than those who never prayed, regardless of class. Working-class people who never prayed seemed slightly *less* superstitious than middle-class people who often prayed. This was the only question on which religion outweighed class as a factor; this in itself suggests that the habit of prayer, of all the aspects of religion, may be the most closely tied up with the superstitions. Unlike, say, a belief in after-life, prayer has a clear role in moments of crisis, panic or anxiety. It often contains an element of placation and fear of authority ('better to be on the right side of God') which differs sharply from the idea of communication between the Shepherd and his flock. It appears that if you are male and middle class, it is very unlikely that you will be superstitious if you never pray; however, if you often pray you are at least as likely to be superstitious as a working-class person who never prays, and nearly as superstitious as a woman who never prays.

Yet things are not as simple as this. About half of those who said they often prayed were unsuperstitious. It may be remembered that about half the number of those who prayed often in private went to church regularly. In fact these two groups were substantially the same people. Of those who often prayed in private, just over half fell into the superstitious groups. However, of those who prayed often *and* went to church regularly, only 20% fell into these groups, compared with 66% of those who prayed often but never went to church. Thus the connection between praying and superstitiousness was completely reversed when praying was associated with regular church attendance. This can only be interpreted as a tribute to the influence of the clergy. It suggests that there is nothing about prayer in itself that tars it with mystifying irrationality, for all depends on whether prayer is moored within a framework of institutional partici-pation. These findings might backfire on a secularist who would use them as ammunition. For it may well be the case that the most orthodox churchgoer *may* be considerably less prone to supersti-tiousness than the most demystified rationalist with an axe to grind. For the former is handed a set of ready-made beliefs, officially approved and stamped, while the latter has to grope in his isolation for his.

Our data cannot take us very far in an evaluation of the extent of religious orthodoxy among churchgoers, or of the real power of the clergy and other ecclesiastical influences in shaping beliefs, attitudes and practices. For *Puzzled People*, less than one-third of its church-going respondents passed its 'test of orthodoxy' (i.e. believed in God, life after death, the Virgin Birth and Christ's Divinity). Belief in Christ's Divinity was actually lower (55%) among churchgoers than among the larger group which believed in God. The proportion of churchgoers believing in the Virgin Birth was similar (56%) to non-churchgoers. Only on life after death was there a significant difference in a direction which would indicate any effective power whatsoever on the part of the church to influence the beliefs of its adherents.[14]

In so far as our findings are comparable, they present a very different picture. Whereas of the total sample, 18% considered religion to be 'very important' in their lives, and 31% believed in life after death, of those who went to church at least once a month, over 60% thought religion 'very important' and believed in an after-life. Nearly three-quarters of these regular churchgoers said they prayed often in private. It would be wrong to place too much reliance on these exact proportions since the number of those attend-ing church is so small. However, the differences are large enough to make the discrepancy with *Puzzled People* glaring. How does one account for this?

Puzzled People points out that 'about one person in ten in Metrop' goes to church 'fairly regularly'. This can be compared with our 15 % who said they go once a month at least. But having quoted this figure, *Puzzled People* then goes on to use a different index in its analysis of orthodoxy, namely the percentage who *have been to church in the last six months*. This may include weddings, christenings and funerals, which are well known to draw the most recalcitrant Christian into church. Using this index, the proportion of regular churchgoers rises from a tenth to nearly a third, and the serious regulars are indistinguishable. It is not surprising that *Puzzled People* concluded that the clergy were so ineffective. We have more positive evidence, although we would emphasize again its statistical inadequacy, that should lead to a reappraisal of the relationship between the church and its congregation.

Under a third of our sample said that they believed in an afterlife, and of the remainder over a third said they were uncertain. When asked if they believed in a God who could intervene in worldly affairs, only 8 % replied that they were uncertain. One can only speculate whether the widespread uncertainty over the possibility of a life to come should be interpreted as a reflection of general apathy over the whole question, or as genuine scepticism. We have no clear notion of what the idea conveys to most people. More than anything the belief may be associated with a general attitude of passive acceptance, perhaps tinged by an optimistic note of compensation. Certainly the accent on retribution and hell-fire has largely disappeared from religious culture in this country – at least where the Church of England is concerned. Accordingly the incentive to adjust one's worldly behaviour, once the principal target of humanist atheists, has largely disappeared. Perhaps the large 'don't know' category indicates that for the majority the issue had become an academic question.

However, this may not be the case. For many people, the idea of 'everything coming to an end' may be totally unacceptable emotionally; ideas of reincarnation and communication with the dead seem to have been widely resuscitated, though such notions are totally foreign to the bodiless bliss of the Christian heaven. What is strikingly absent from such notions, however, is the idea of religious responsibility. This might be the key to their relationship with superstitious beliefs and practices like astrology and spiritualism. The latter 'science' is a practical means of keeping in touch through the use of neutral media. Similarly reincarnation is an automatic 'natural' process – nature does not discriminate, or send people to different places. The atmosphere of the Balance Book is missing. Hence, subjectively, the intellectual inhibitions which might have obstructed the belief in an after life from being assimilated to superstitions have been largely eroded. Objectively, the power of the clergy to reassert them is limited by dwindling congregations, although where its influence does extend, it appears to be largely successful.

The fact that the belief was held by two-thirds of the regular churchgoers may reflect this success. Of those who believed in an after-life 28% were regular churchgoers, while the latter were in a minority of only 15% in the total sample. While *Puzzled People* found that nearly half those who attended Church of England services either disbelieved or were uncertain about life after death, the proportion of believers among our churchgoers was almost double that among those who professed a belief in God.

Disregarding this distinction for the moment, the figures revealed a significant correlation between belief in an after-life and superstitiousness. Among both men and women of both classes those who believed tended to be more superstitious than those who did not, with the proviso that, overall, men tended to be less superstitious than women, and middle-class less than working-class, regardless of belief.

Of those who believed in an after-life, 51% were to be found in the superstitious groups, compared with 42% for the whole sample. However, the belief was not related *per se* with a high level of superstitiousness. The crucial factor was, again, whether or not it was associated with regular church attendance. Sixty-three per cent of those who held the belief but never went to church fell into the superstitious groups, compared with only 20% of those believers who said they attended church at least once a month. If church attendance is held constant, the association between religious belief and superstitiousness becomes even more striking among those who never attend.

It is probable that where the influence of the clergy does not extend, the moral content of the idea of a life after death is eroded and lost to vague notions of all kinds. It is possible to see the success of

E

spiritualism as a brilliant exploitation of this confusion by the importation of a 'scientific' method which promises to yield practical results. Again, there is widespread evidence of the increasing popularity of notions of reincarnation, and many interesting 'syntheses' of Eastern and Western religions which make good money out of processing their adherents into irresistible and unbearable personalities. Where once an articulated religious framework existed, a hierarchy of concepts which reflected an immutable heavenly scheme in which a man had clear duties and sublime rewards, an overnight market has sprung up. When instant superhuman powers are promised and advertised on stickers in the Tube, the distinction between a religion and a superstitious belief becomes an issue of interest to academics and clerics alone.

Conclusions

In this article we have described and analysed the results of a survey into various sorts of metaphysical beliefs and ideas. For a number of reasons, already explained, some caution is necessary in the interpretation of the results. Nevertheless, in an area which is still relatively uncharted, we felt that the results of even a small pilot survey might be of general interest.

Our findings have reinforced the view that superstition and allied beliefs in Britain today do present a problem for sociologists. In a society which is commonly regarded as increasingly dominated by scientific, rational criteria, why are superstitious ideas still familiar and, amongst a small percentage of the population, apparently believed in?

Before discussing this question it might be helpful to summarize the principal findings which we have discussed above. While a large minority of our sample paid at least lip-service to the common superstitions, about 6–8% appeared to 'really believe' in them. Between 9% and 23% appeared to believe in astrology, while about one-third subscribed to the principal religious beliefs and appeared to care about them at least to the extent of praying regularly and saying that religion was fairly important to them. Women were consistently more superstitious and more religious than men except for the fact that men seemed more likely to believe in 'luck'. There were no consistent class differences in subscription to the common superstitions, though working-class people were much more inclined to read the horoscopes and to believe in 'luck'. The reader may notice an apparent contradiction here with the findings discussed in the section on 'Religion and Superstitiousness', where a significant class relationship *was* found. This was due to the weight given to astrology questions when constructing the 'superstitious' scores. Broadly speaking, the old and the young were less sceptical than those in the middle age groups.

Many different explanations have been suggested as to why we are still superstitious. Each one is probably partially true, though not surprisingly none can give a sufficient explanation. The range of activities and beliefs commonly described as superstitious are too varied to allow a simple explanation.

Some psychologists see superstition as the result of 'mistaken learning'. Two events which are not in fact linked together, for example, success in the pools entry posted immediately after the appearance of a black cat, are causally associated in the mind as a result of experience.[15] A variant of this theory suggests that a well-known superstition, particularly if enshrined in an aphorism, causes people to observe the world selectively and notice only those events which support the belief. Again, superstition can be explained as a temporary reversion, caused by anxiety, to infantile beliefs in magic and animism.[16] These theories, though interesting in themselves, cannot explain the social patterning of superstitious behaviour, for instance, that women are more superstitious than men or that working-class people tend to read and 'believe in' astrology more than middle-class people.

Moving towards more sociological explanations, superstition can be seen as a form of alienation. One can argue that beliefs in fate and luck, while helping people to come to terms with a harsh world, in fact conceal the true causes of their situation; they therefore provide a sort of safety-valve between suffering and complaint or revolt. The evidence tends to support the view that maxims such as 'better to be born lucky than rich' are more popular amongst the working class than amongst the middle class. Nevertheless, it does seem likely that only a minority of the working class now hold such views. For example, of our working-class respondents, very nearly one half said that the world was definitely not a fair place. Moreover, it is difficult to accommodate this theory with the fact that women are more superstitious than men.

Alternatively, one can interpret superstition as a means and expression of social solidarity. According to this view the significance of the belief content of the superstition is minimized; the important part is the form of words which expresses it. Phrases such as 'disasters always come in threes' or 'never look at a new moon through glass' are seen not so much as part of the ideology of a group but rather as an element in its particular language. Hoggart says of working-class people: 'They may appear to have views on general matters – on religion, on politics, and so on – but these views usually prove to be a bundle of largely unexamined and orally transmitted tags, enshrining generalizations, prejudices, and half-truths, and elevated by epigrammatic phrasing into the status of maxims.'[17] Thus people derive a 'cosy sense of belongingness' when members of their group use such phrases at certain predictable times. A problem or fear can be satisfactorily dealt with by an idea which sounds both cheerful and final and with which nobody in the group is likely to disagree. In this way we can interpret the relatively frequent use of the phrase 'touch wood' (e.g. 'I haven't had a cold yet this winter, touch wood') as little more than an idiom of speech which makes the whole sentence sound acceptable.

However, despite the dangers of over-intellectualizing superstition, one must eventually come back to the content of these beliefs. Many superstititions appear to have existed for centuries, during most of which time they have been condemned by the official creed. It would seem unlikely that they would have survived so long if they did not fulfil some particular function for individuals in addition to those already suggested. So we come to a final explanation for their existence and survival which is that they are believed in, to a greater or lesser extent, either consciously or unconsciously, by those who pay lip-service to them. This theory assumes that people tend to search for satisfactory and meaningful explanations of events in the world; they also perhaps want to be able to control and predict events – even such trivial ones as the arrival of a bus. Inevitably there are gaps between these desires and what is in fact possible. Thus one can explain superstition as the 'God of the Gaps'. If science cannot provide satisfactory answers to questions like 'Why should this happen to me?', perhaps superstititition can: 'Disasters always come in threes', or 'Don't forget you saw a magpie *and* a black cat and you were bragging only a short time ago about how splendid everything in your life was.' Many questions of this type cannot be answered by science, so to the extent that this theory is true there is little reason to expect superstitition to decline with advancing knowledge. Malinowski observed that his Trobriand Islanders were more likely to resort to magic in circumstances which they were unable to control by any other means. One can argue that, despite the enormous development of scientific and technical knowledge, a similar principle is at work in twentieth-century Britain.

There seems to be good evidence that superstitious practices increase in time of anxiety, for example during a war. We also found that a number of people who were usually non-religious, in some cases actually atheistic, had often prayed during the war. These may have been 'little prayers', indicating no more positive belief than do curses, but in many cases they may indicate an element of belief which returned to the forefront of the mind when all else had failed. Again there is evidence that people look to astrology for encouragement when they are worried or depressed. Thus one can argue that both superstitious practices and private prayer reduce anxiety, albeit in a very small way, and that this is an important reason for their survival. People need a 'God of the Gaps' most when they are worried.

Following on from this one would expect those people who are least able to control their situation to be most superstititious. One can argue that women are more superstitious because their situation is to a considerable extent outside their own control. Moreover, this is particularly true amongst working-class people whose life situation is anyway fairly insecure. The women need the security most because they have to feed and rear the children yet there is little they can do to obtain it except rely on their husbands.[18]

Again one can argue that working-class people are less able to control what happens to them than middle-class people, whose favourable social situation is often enhanced by greater knowledge and skills. If this generalization is broadly correct one would expect working-class people to be more superstitious. Our findings suggest that they are much more likely than middle-class people to 'believe in' astrology and in notions of fate and luck. Perhaps the fact that there is no consistent class difference in subscription to the common superstitions suggests that these are less important as a means of allaying anxiety.

It is significant that the superstitious practices common in Britain today interfere hardly, if at all, with the course of people's normal life. It is probable that the lack of an "opportunity cost" is one reason why people still obey the prescriptions: 'It's no trouble to do it and, though it seems silly, well, it just might be true so why not?' Similar explanations can be given of private religious beliefs and prayer.

This brings us to the question of the relationship between superstition and religion. The analysis in the section above suggests the tentative conclusion that religious belief, when not associated with active membership of a church, tends to be associated with superstitious belief while church attendance tends to be antithetical to superstition. Moreover, we have some evidence that for those people who do not got to church but yet say they are religious and pray often, religious belief has moved quite far from the orthodox church position and is really much closer to what would normally be called superstition. If this view is correct, it would seem that there is a gulf between orthodox religion on the one hand and superstition and private religion on the other which really makes it impossible to describe the latter as just a variant of the former.

Postcript

What implications does our evidence, such as it is, have for the argument about secularization? To a considerable extent the significance of superstitious practices in this argument turns on the definitions of 'secularity' and 'rationality'. Though the definition of secularization as the replacement of metaphysical ideas in general is at least as old as Engels, the social and cultural domination of Christianity in England, and of the Church of England in particular, has tended to narrow discussion. Defined negatively in terms of the decline of religious institutions, the concept of secularization used to be relatively free of problems. Whether in fact the Reformation represented secularization – as the replacement of other-worldliness by elements of this-worldliness in a religious culture that was simultaneously revitalized – was indeed problematical, but religious history since has minimized the importance of these problems. For despite the existence of denominational minorities, the overlap of creed and practice was considerable and there were few conversions. Hence the process of secularization could be measured relatively simply by the decline of specifically Christian beliefs, practices and institutions and there is no doubt that secularization in this *ad hoc* sense has occurred.

However, secularization was rarely taken to mean only the decline in religious institutions and belief. It was a positive theory that the 'new method', based on scepticism, empirical investigation, analysis and strict reasoning could provide an adequate account of the world, a good explanation of physical and social events, and a satisfactory, and satisfying, basis for both social organization and individual action. Further, its inherent superiority would result in the refutation and rejection of all religious, metaphysical and superstitious ideas, *and hence* the destruction of patterns of behaviour or organization based on these ideas. For different reasons, Marx and Engels predicted the same end. Religious and superstitious beliefs were seen as forms of human alienation, whereby real, worldly processes are represented and protected by metaphysical forms. 'Rationalism' was an ideology more appropriate to the existing social conditions, an analysis that would aid the victory in social conflict of the class that used it. But only the advent of Socialism would remove the social alienation which metaphysical belief represented. In the meantime, social change would expose the function in social control of the old beliefs, and those which no longer rested on any social foundation would be eroded.

Since it is now universally agreed that institutional religion has declined in Britain, attention is focused on secularization defined in some more general sense. It is at this point that we should consider the relationship between secularity and rationality. It will be remembered that 'rational' was the key word used by Wilson to describe 'secular' society in the quotation at the beginning of this article. Both terms have been used in our discussion of superstition.

Though frequently confused in practice, the two concepts are logically distinct. Assuming the goals of an action to be arbitrary, 'rationality' is a way of describing the procedure by which those goals are attained, i.e. the most effective adjustment of means to ends. The term 'secular', on the other hand is used to classify goals themselves. Thus it is possible to conceive of an increasing process of rationality not only within belief systems that are secular in their entirety, but also within those which are totally unsecular.

There is often confusion about the units that are 'rational' or 'secular'. Wilson talks about a 'secular society', Martin about 'secular people'. The two need not be the same. Alasdair MacIntyre quotes an eighteenth-century divine as saying 'I know of no case where the maxim "in Godliness there is great gain" has greater applicability than in the management of an extensive factory'.[19]

He clearly envisaged a society in which the majority of people (the working class at least) were religious, but yet society as a whole was organized for the highly secular goal of private profit.

A society can be secular in various ways. For instance, it can be secular because its members are secular. Or it can be secular because it values things that are 'real' (wealth for instance, rather than salvation) and values them for their own sakes, rather than as a means to an ultimately metaphysical goal. When it comes to individual beliefs and actions, the form and scope of the concept may be different. Religion, for example, has made many statements of fact that have been proved incorrect; scientific methodology at present has not yet provided an adequate account of many significant empirical phenomena, most notably social causation; unreason has been shown to be of immense psychological and social significance, and may well be indispensable; it is a philosophical truism that empirical methods cannot give an adequate account of ethics or questions of ultimate value. All these layers can yield a concept of secularization. One person may account as secular 'the keeping of religion in its place', for instance the winnowing of 'spiritual truth' from factual error in the bible. Another may insist on scepticism where science has not to date provided an explanation.

A description of the possible scope of secularization does not solve the problem of finding a criterion, but it shows that what criterion is adopted must depend on the analytical category one is concerned with. The first task is to demarcate the latter. Our working definition was concerned with the empirical sphere, and to a slight extent with social causation. We were interested if beliefs were nonsense in terms of science either because they predicted absurd patterns or forms of causation or because they referred to agencies or principles of no scientific status.

But even with this narrow definition there are still difficulties in practice in deciding what is secular. One criterion is adherence to ideas that are considered to be true, as opposed to false or meaningless. This definition derives from Pareto, but it has considerable problems. While it does provide a basis for comparison between one culture and another, it assumes that the reasons for incorrect belief are everywhere the same. Invoking Gods or spirits is treated similarly to inadequate knowledge and technique. Secondly it invokes a spurious determinacy of secularization, since it is our science that is the test, and the past has led, willy-nilly to the present. A second attempt of the same sort is to indicate as 'superstitious' any idea that is out of line, in the light of the knowledge of the day. But while this does enable units of discussion to be identified within one culture, it renders unintelligible any attempts at comparison. In an extreme case increasing intellectual homogeneity would count as secularization. If *we*, however are to judge what beliefs were reasonable, some, not very good, measure of secularization could result. However, what is counted as 'true' or 'correct' or 'reasonable' is difficult.

The marxist concept of alienation would present an additional problem here. Belief in fate is usually considered a metaphysical belief, but for most people outside the middle and upper classes the recognition that the pattern of life is largely beyond the control of individuals or even groups is surely only a recognition of fact. Thus belief in fate is secular and non-secular at the same time. The belief corresponds to secular facts, but is non-secular in its individual manifestations. An idea can also be 'true' in the scientific sense, but believed in for the wrong reasons. One woman who appeared to have no metaphysical belief answered a series of our questions as follows: 'Have you ever consulted an astrologer?' – 'No.' 'A Palmist?' – 'No.' 'A fortune-teller?' – 'No.' 'Anyone else like that?' – 'Only the doctor.' Just as a metaphysical idea may have more logic than is immediately apparent, so a belief does not necessarily become secular because its content is co-terminous with rational, secular and well-informed opinion. In fact all people nearly all the time have had to rely on authority for information on which to base their lives. The scepticism characteristic of secularity is now, as always, the luxury of the privileged few with the time and energy to pursue it. Is the man who believes what he is told secular or not? The ordinary man has not more chance now than before the scientific revolution of checking for himself the beliefs he must accept. There has been a change in the type of experts that are respected; but this may reflect the better quality of their miracles rather than more intellectual discrimination.

Another problem is presented by the person who assents to apparently metaphysical propositions on grounds that owe much to secular methodology. There is the person who scoffed at the idea that bad luck ran in threes, until three of his kin died in close succession, there being no apparent link, or the person who did not believe in ghosts until he saw one. There will normally be convincing ways of disposing of this 'evidence'. However, the mental processes of these people will owe more to secular scepticism than many a person who blindly follows conventional science. For one of the characteristics of a secular person is intellectual individualism, and a reluctance to take on trust what he is told. Given the range of human capacities mistakes will proliferate, so that ideas may be wider off the mark in a society of such people than in a society with a secular élite and a population of faithful devotees.

Obviously the problem of defining 'secularity' is too complex to allow an easy solution; no doubt it will tease sociologists and philosophers for many years to come. Even if it could be established fairly conclusively that certain practices and attitudes are common in Britain today, there would still be disagreement as to whether this 'fact' indicated that our society was more or less secular than, for example, Bryan Wilson has argued.

In addition to the conceptual problems any attempt to obtain satisfactory information on the subject runs into massive methodological difficulties. We did not attempt to make our sample representative and hence are not trying to draw any conclusions about the general nature of English society. We did, however, try to make the very difficult jump from recording a person's outward behaviour to estimating its 'inner significance' for him. In many cases our efforts took us no further than recognition of the difficulties involved in making this jump. We did not find on the whole that people were reluctant to talk about these inner beliefs. On the contrary, many people were obviously interested in the questions and would like to have been able to discuss them at length. However, they were often unable to do this because they did not understand our questions or because they were unable to articulate their own ideas. In answer to the questions probing for explanations of behaviour or belief, people frequently said that they had 'never really thought about it before' and one felt that this was the main reason why they did not say very much. Furthermore, interviewers, particularly student interviewers, vary in their ability to draw forth and write down significant comments. There is also bound to be disagreement among social scientists about the significance of any coherent statements that are obtained from respondents. However, despite all these difficulties and despite many disagreements on other points, we remain convinced that some investigation of the beliefs and attitudes behind actions should form a principal part in any discussion about the secularity of our society. We hope that our description of a pilot survey in this field will help to suggest the lines along which such research might be planned.

NOTES

1. David Martin, *The Religious and the Secular*, Routledge and Kegan Paul 1969, pp. 107 ff.
2. Bryan Wilson, *Religion in Secular Society*, Watts and Co. 1966, p. x.
3. Judd Marmor, 'Some reflections on Superstitions in Contemporary Life', *American Journal of Orthopsychiatry*, 1956, p. 119.
4. Kenneth Garwood, 'Superstition and Half Belief', *New Society*, 31 January 1963.
5. Alisdair MacIntyre, *Secularization and Moral Change*, OUP 1967, p. 17.
6. Richard Hoggart, *The Uses of Literacy*, Penguin Books 1962, p. 29.
7. The reader is referred to certain studies which deal with problems similar to ours:
   (i) Geoffrey Gorer, *Exploring English Character*, Cresset Press 1955, Chapter 14.
   (ii) Opinion Research Centre article in *The Sunday Times* 5 April 1968.
   (iii) British Institute of Public Opinion, unpublished material.
8. Geoffrey Gorer, op. cit.
9. Opinion Research Centre, op. cit.
10. Judd Marmor, op. cit.
11. David Martin, op. cit., p. 106.
12. Mass Observation, *Puzzled People*, Victor Gollancz 1948.
13. Ibid., pp. 59 ff.
14. Ibid., p. 27 and pp. 42 ff.
15. Cf. Gustav Jahoda, *The Psychology of Superstition*, Allen Lane The Penguin Press 1969, pp. 74 ff.
16. Cf. ibid., pp. 102 ff.
17. Richard Hoggart, op. cit., p. 103.
18. Cf. Michael Young and Peter Wilmott, *Family and Kinship in East London*, Routledge and Kegan Paul p. 189. (Also available in Penguin Books.)
19. Alisdair MacIntyre, op. cit., p. 19.

8 Education, Secularization, Desecularization and Resecularization

*Margaret Scotford Archer
and Michalina Vaughan*

THE integration of education with a plurality of social institutions is predominantly a characteristic of complex industrial societies, since history shows education otherwise to have been relatively autonomous. In traditional and pre-industrial societies, education was mainly monopolized by religion, as learning was identified with the transmission of religious knowledge; the degree to which education and religion were integrated varied directly with the extent to which a religion relied on written documents and with the complexity of its internal organization. There are some instances of the multiple integration of education not only with religion but also with other social institutions. Such integration coincided with the interpenetration of religious and secular élites, so that we have, for example, tripartite connections between the Brahmins, education and caste or between the Mandarins, education and administration. Nevertheless, despite these historical instances which include religion, modern theorists have argued that in industrial societies, the increased institutional integration of education is inseparable from the decline and ultimate exclusion of its former integration with religion. This argument is expressed, explicitly or implicitly, in three complementary statements about education:

1. Secularization is inevitable.
2. Desecularization is improbable.
3. Resecularization is unavoidable.

1. *The inevitability of secularization*

While the theory of the inevitable secularization of education has gained wide uncritical acceptance, it is not to be found in a single agreed form. Three main types of explanation can be distinguished, each of which points to a causal mechanism, a 'logic' which necessarily implies the decline of religious control over education and of its symbolic content. The following table summarizes the three types of theory which seem to underpin the common generalizations.

Theory type	Process	Educational change
A. Idealist	Increasing rationality leads to demand for secular-rational education according to the *logic of rationalism*	Zero-sum of reason-religion reflected in education
B. Structuralist	Increasing industrial complexity leads to need for secular instrumental education according to the *logic of industrialism*	Institutional adaptation to secular socio-economic needs
C. Dialectical	Interaction of ideas and institutions, as the economy diversifies and rationality grows. Leads to secular instrumental education according to the *logic of complementarity*	Institutional secularization as needs and desires converge

Theory type A

The common denominator of the theories in the first group is the view that institutional organization is culturally determined; it is most marked in the thought of philosophical evolutionists like Condorcet and Comte. These theories tend to be idealist, seeing changes in thought-process as the exclusive or major causes of institutional change. Having assumed a zero-sum relationship between reason and religion, they see increases in rationality as necessarily leading to institutional secularization. It is argued that the diffusion of rational ideas through the population will automatically result in a growing demand for secular instruction and hence in the gradual transformation of educational provisions. Thus, for philosophical evolutionists, the 'logic of rationalism' implies the inevitability of institutional secularization.

The least complex monocausal theory is that of Condorcet. He maintains that the spread of enlightenment corresponds to a simultaneous decline in religious prejudice. Throughout history, human progress has been restricted by tendentious religious teachings, and each epoch has been the scene of a struggle between superstition and reason. Progress in society, defined by the extent to which the natural rights of all its members are safeguarded, can never occur unless the people are emancipated by enlightenment from the domination of ambitious minorities pursuing sectional interests.[1] Among populations dominated by prejudice, philosophy is subjugated by political considerations and reduced to ideologies justifying self-interest and expediency, whereas in an enlightened society philosophy (rationality) will shape institutions positively.

> All institutions according to Condorcet owed their existence to 'opinion': the bad ones to 'prejudice', or perverted opinion; and the good ones to 'reason', or enlightened opinion.[2]

This cultural determinism assumes as a fact that secularization by enlightened public demand is inevitable – a process of which the French Revolution was presented as the outcome and of which Condorcet's own plan for a secular educational system was to him merely a corollary. Comte owes much to Condorcet's evolutionism, but 'refines' the latter's logic of rationalism in postulating that certain structural factors may stimulate the dissemination of the positive spirit. The industrial age represents a quest for physical laws which is the exact opposite of reliance on Providence, and while not initiating it, will further institutional secularization.

Such theories have the advantage that they account for the occurrence of secular educational systems in pre-industrial societies, e.g. eighteenth-century revolutionary legislation in France and similar provisions currently adopted in some under-developed countries. However, they offer no explanation for countries like England and Germany, which retained the religious control and the religious content of education after having developed an industrial economy. This divergence could only be attributed to a lesser diffusion of rationalism among the population – an assumption which could not be substantiated by any form of evidence and which directly contradicts the complementarity postulated by Comte between industrialization and enlightenment.

Theory type B

It has often been assumed, quite apart from the development of a broad theoretical framework, that there is a causal relation between industrial and educational secularization. An example of this approach can be found in Bryan Wilson's statement:

> As knowledge itself became increasingly secular so priests became less appropriate as teachers, and as the content of education shifted from a religious-moral concern (developed at least partially in the interests of the maintenance of social control) to an increasingly instrumental-technical concern (developed in the interest of increased economic productivity), so education emerged into an institutional order in its own right.[3]

It is, however, the theoretical framework of structural functionalism, with its concentration on institutional adaptation to social needs, which fully specifies the 'logic of industrialism'. To Parsons, education

> functions to internalize in its pupils both the commitments and capacities for the successful performance of their future adult roles, and . . . functions to allocate these human resources within the role structure of the adult society.[4]

Hence structural factors are seen as constituting the independent variable. The influence of educationalists as individuals or within pressure groups is explicitly subordinated to structural change:

> The growth in specialization of schools was, therefore, a response to social needs. The form which education took was influenced by the educationalists, but within the limits set by the existing social framework. Frequently the ideas of pioneers have only been influential after their death, once social conditions have changed in a direction which has made them relevant.[5]

Among the specific requirements which industrialization imposes upon education is commonly included the inculcation of rational and materialistic values.

However, different rates of industrialization and the predicted degree of institutional adaptation in education do not in fact correspond. Thus while on a multiplicity of indices (the percentage of manpower engaged in industry, contribution of industrial production to GNP, number or size of factories) nineteenth-century England outdistanced France, yet it was the latter whose educational institutions bore the characteristics attributed to industrial societies, i.e. specialized training for the professions and administration, increased social mobility through school achievement, rationalistic educational philosophy and a secular curriculum. Even though functionalist theory can provide explanations for delayed institutional adaptation to structural requirements in the English case, it is logically incapable of accounting for the educational 'pre-adaptation' of the French system.

The reasons for slow institutional adaptation can be located in the past (the partial endurance of superseded 'traditions'), in the present (structural discontinuities of society) or in the future (a period of transition to a new equilibrium). The first explanation makes use of the idea of institutional cultural lags and involves the admission that the endurance of traditional cultural values can inhibit adaptation. However, the label 'traditional' does not suggest a transient nature, nor does it provide any indication of the possible duration of the alleged lag. Explanations employing the idea of a cultural lag are essentially *post hoc*, since their account seems to confuse present evaluations of historical institutions and ideas with an objective analysis of their contemporary influence and its subsequent effect. Similarly, the stress on cultural discontinuities or periods of transition (the two are logically, but not empirically, distinguishable) again lacks specific predictive power. It depends for its statement of ultimate institutional adaptation upon a confusion between trends and laws. Such a theory admits that specific conditions can influence adaptation, yet depends for its validity upon the eventual disappearance of these conditions. In fact, traditionalistic groups continue to function as interest groups, influencing institutional development, after their economic or ideological supremacy has been challenged. The deposition of such a group from a previous position of domination does not spell its ultimate decline or automatically deprive its source of legitimation of all future appeal. It will tend to continue for as long as participation offers its members either objective or subjective advantages. As an interest group, it will interact with others and influence educational institutions, even if it fails to dominate them. If institutional adaptation is not unavoidable, secularization is not inevitable either.

Theory type C

The third type of theory considers it 'as axiomatic that a historical phenomenon of such scope (as secularization) will not be amenable to any monocausal explanations', counter-claiming that 'the dialectical relationship between religion and society thus precludes the doctrinaire approaches of either "idealism" or "materialism".'[6] Rather, the mechanism leading to secularization, defined (significantly) as a joint sociocultural process, is the constant interaction of ideas and institutions, psychological and social factors. Or, stated in most general terms, it is the interaction of structure and culture in the world of everyday praxis.

Theories type A and B both pointed to a convergence between structure and culture, the supply of and demand for certain educational institutions, and in each case one factor was given a fundamental place. Thus, in type A the specific variable was designated as an 'enlightened élite' (Condorcet and Comte) which preceded and prompted the definition and establishment of educational institutions. Once organized, supply (according to this type) stimulates further demand and the productivity generated by output enables reinvestment in terms of increased supply: structure and culture converge to reinforce each other.[7] In type B, the institutions founded in accordance with dominant economic needs of the economy will embody the instrumental economic requirements, eventually stimulating a universal demand for such education. As demand tends towards universality, supply converges in the foundation of a national educational system. Berger avoids infrastructural/superstructural imputations, and endorses a dialectical process of causation which gives rise to a correlation between structure and culture in which 'the manifestation of secularization on the level of consciousness ("subjective secularization", if one wishes) has its correlate on the social structural level (as "objective secularization" '.[8]

When we deal with specific historical occurrences of secularization, however, Berger argues that we must 'trace' the dialectic throughout the different parts of the time sequence. In analysing Western Protestantism and secularization, he clearly separates the causes of the origins of the phenomenon from the cause of its continuation. The origins are multiple, apart from various structural factors, Protestantism contributing the seeds of its own 'destruction', but the cause for continuation is single, and located in the process of industrialization:

A modern industrial society requires the presence of large cadres of scientific and technical personnel, whose training and ongoing organization presupposes a high degree of rationalization, not only on the level of infrastructure but also on that of consciousness. Any attempts at traditionalistic reconquista thus threaten to dismantle the rational foundations of modern society. Furthermore, the secularizing potency of capitalistic-industrial rationalization is not only self-perpetuating but self-aggrandizing.[9]

Thus the 'logic of industrialism' reasserts itself and religion, together

with traditional sources of legitimation, 'under the impact of secularization can, indeed, be analysed convincingly as a "dependent
variable" today'.[10] Rationality and industrialization are so inextricably linked that:

> one may say, with only some exaggeration, that economic data on industrial
> productivity or capital expansion can predict the religious crisis of credibility
> in a particular society more easily than data derived from the 'history of ideas'
> of that society.[11]

Not only are historical variations in philosophy largely irrelevant
to the process and rate of secularization; so, too, are contemporary
differences in the organization of industrial production. Thus 'the
logic of industrialism' becomes universal for the developed world
and the structural imperatives of production are the sufficient conditions of further secularization.

> Today, it would seem, it is industrial society in itself that is secularizing, with
> its divergent ideological legitimations serving merely as modification of the
> global secularization process.[12]

Yet Berger seems well aware of the imperfections of this 'logic'
when used to interpret past history. The relative immunity of the
religiously legitimated state to long-standing industrialization
can hardly be attributed to the differential impact of industry or
to 'cultural lag' which tends to be used to account for continued
religious practice in the family, particularly in the context of the
planned economy. More importantly, the pre-industrial secular
French state and education system is admitted to run counter to the
'tendency toward the secularization of the political order that goes
naturally with the development of modern industrialism'.[13] Such
exceptions lower not only the explanatory power but also, automatically, the predictive power of the theory which seeks to extend
the Western prototype elsewhere.

> It appears that the same secularizing forces have now become world wide in
> the course of westernization and modernization.[14]

Since in the past, specific conditions preceding or accompanying
industrialization have influenced the religious or non-religious nature
of social institutions both in terms of their control and symbolic
'content', there is no reason to expect that these conditions will have
no effect in the future.

Thus the three types of theory with their variations in the themes of the 'logic of rationalism' and the 'logic of industrialism' have pointed to decisive trends in the secularization of education. Since exceptions to the rule can be cited for all the 'logics', however, they retain the status of trends, not laws.

2. *The improbability of desecularization*

All of the three types of theory put forward a secondary proposition which remains immune from any criticism levelled at the idea of the inevitability of secularization, namely, that once the secularizing process *has* occurred in a given institution, it will tend to be irreversible. The two processes of increased rationalization and progressive industrialization will, it is argued, intensify 'resistance' to religious control or sacred symbolism in social institutions throughout their development, and therefore change in the form of reversion will become increasingly unlikely. However, since types A and B compound the cause of origin with the cause of continued secularization, whereas type C distinguishes between the two, we find a strong and a weak statement respectively of 'the improbability of desecularization'.

Theory type A

By stressing a unilinear advance of society and its component institutions, and confounding development with progress, the philosophical evolutionists in this category present the strongest statement of the irreversibility of secularization *vis à vis* education. Since both Comte and Condorcet regarded increased rationality as the mechanism which guarantees evolution, and since education is given the key role of ensuring its diffusion and universalization, any recognition of the potential or possible desecularization of instruction would have implied the collapse of the theory. Thus the 'plausibility of religion' will be lower in educational instruction than in any other institution, and incapable of resurgence. Enlightenment itself, and the manifest advantages – both material and intellectual – that it confers on society and the individual alike, is the mechanism preceding desecularization.

Theory type B

Those who claim that social institutions are superstructural and that the economy is determined infrastructurally, together with those who stress that technology is the prime factor in defining the content of education, again view the increase of the element of science in instruction as both inevitable and irreversible. However, the emphasis on scientific subjects in the curriculum does not automatically exclude other subjects. (It is interesting to note that in Marx's mechanistic infrastructure, industrialization will increase the instrumental-vocational content of education, without reducing the religious false consciousness which is disseminated through instruction for purposes of social control.) Nevertheless, once an instrumental-vocational education has been initiated, its relevance to maintaining and expanding industrial production by spreading technical and administrative skills will receive almost universal acknowledgment. The closer the association between education and occupation, the greater will become the demand for the type of instruction geared to social promotion. Thus any pressures for traditionalistic curricula will be opposed not only by industrial interests on economic grounds, but also by popular demand on social grounds. In addition, the more authority relies on rational sources of legitimation and on financial incentives, the more religion will be represented as an inferior form of social control. As the process of industrialization expands and is seen to have unlimited prospects, the likelihood of desecularization automatically decreases.

Theory type C

This type contains a similar, though weaker, statement of the necessary continuation of secularization, since the

> 'liberated territory' of secularized sectors of society is so centrally 'located', in and around the capitalist-industrialist economy, that any attempt to 'reconquer' it in the name of religio-political-traditionalism endangers the continued functioning of this economy.[15]

Thus, only if the cause of the continuation of the phenomenon were suspended, that is, if the course of industrialization were halted, could desecularization theoretically occur. This possibility is allowed in the statement that while

> The same complex is international (today just about world-wide), it becomes increasingly difficult to isolate any particular national society from its rationalizing effects without at the same time keeping that society in a condition of economic backwardness.[16]

However, as Berger claims that the processes of Westernization and modernization have now become global and that the necessary condition of desecularization is a reversion to a pre-industrial economy, reversal of the secularizing trend is in practice a virtual impossibility.

Thus the three types of theory have pointed to either the theoretical impossibility (A and B) or the extreme practical unlikelihood (C) of institutional desecularization. However, to dispute A and B requires only the production of a single counter-example of institutional desecularization, whereas to challenge C requires evidence of the non-rarity of the phenomenon (however this would be assessed). It is our contention that at least two types of counter-example showing institutional desecularization may be cited, i.e. cases of national independence movements and of counter-revolution (though there might be some justification for considering the former as a special case of the latter.)

While examples of a religious group regaining actual *control* over an educational system can be found, they do tend to be less frequent and further back in the past than cases where a religious *content* to instruction is reintroduced. Weber's discussion of types of authority and of the varying sources of the legitimation of a group not only admits the possibility of desecularization, but also helps to account for its concentration on the symbolic level. Since in time each initial type of legitimation may be replaced or supplemented by either of the other two, in certain circumstances a rational-legal form may give way to a religio-traditionalistic one. If it is admitted that the complete transformation of the rational-legal form is less frequent than that of the other two types, it follows that a group suffering a crisis of legitimacy is more likely to supplement the rational-legal with others than to replace it by them. Because of its capacity to introduce the new or additional source, the educational system is almost by definition the social institution most affected. An almost classical example is the attempt of the English Utilitarians and the group they represented to legitimate the system of authority in industrial production by the inculcation of classical economic tenets in education. When this policy proved less than successful, Kay-Shuttleworth proposed the reintroduction of religion, with its concentration on a man's station in life, at the primary level.[17] Thus, even if one were restricted to cases of supplementary legitimation where religious symbolism was reincorporated into secular instruction, this instance would be sufficient to indicate the possibility of institutional desecularization.

However, to admit this possibility is not to damage the contention of theory type C that nevertheless the empirical frequency of (educational) desecularization will be low. A comparison of the conditions attending independence movements and counter-revolutions which reintroduced religion into instruction with similar groups which did not, may make possible both an initial specification of the optimal conditions for desecularization and the enumeration of grounds for assessing their frequency of occurrence. While a rough inspection of a number of cases yields a hypothetical scheme of the optimal conditions under which certain types of religion are reintroduced into institutions, these cannot be considered as necessary conditions, since various degrees of coercive power at the disposal of the dominant group can render them dispensable. Thus they represent a preliminary and crude attempt to specify the types of situation in which religion may be used once more to legitimate established *authority*.

1. It would seem to be an advantage for the 'psychologically liberated' group, previously dominating a secular educational system, to be small in relation to a relatively less enlightened population. While this situation is obviously characteristic of the highly stratified pre-industrial society (the typical *ancien régime*), it would also include the 'closed' industrial social structure with a bifurcated educational system producing a trained élite and a large, relatively undifferentiated body of loyal citizens, as well as the 'colonized territory' in which the governing power had provided secular instruction for the few, whether by educating the élite of the pre-colonial hierarchy or by instituting its own selection procedures. The implication is not that, given the chance to overthrow the élite, the 'unenlightened' will simply revert, but rather that the small size of the élite will make it easier to discredit them and the existence of an alternative value system among the non-élite will provide not only a source of unity, but also a 'rationale' by which the discrediting will be done.

Thus, for example, the enlightened leaders of the Third Estate, who in the three Revolutionary Assemblies had legislated for a secular educational system, confiscated church schools and forbidden the religious orders to teach, could be discredited (in this sphere) on largely religious grounds by Napoleon.[18] (Interestingly, his own Université Imperiale suffered the same fate at the hands of the Restauration, which reinstated religious control over instructions at all levels.) Similarly, the North African élite, trained in secular French schools, detached from Islamic culture and religion and awarded key posts between the wars, were branded as 'Blancs-noirs' by the growing independence movements[19] and condemned on religious and cultural grounds. Again, the growth of Indian nationalism in the nineteen-twenties was accompanied by a condemnation of Western materialism, an increased appreciation of the oriental classics, an accentuation of Eastern spiritual values and the revival of religious cults all culminating in Tagore's criticism of Western utilitarian values in education and Gandhi's defence of Hinduism against Christian materialism.[20] The unenlightened non-élite thus represents a disadvantaged group whose traditionalistic value-system can legitimate their bid for control and for increased participation, and may influence subsequent policy if they are successful.

However, a fairly frequent occurrence among colonial independence movements is that while religious appeals may be made consistently throughout the fight, they often receive only minor institutional application. Witness, for instance, the virtual continuation of the metropolitan educational system in North Africa, with only the cultural and linguistic aspects of 'Arabization' being introduced.[21] These cases tend to occur in situations where the immediate production of technical and administrative personnel appears vital to bureaucratic efficiency and economic productivity.

2. Thus the second condition favourable to desecularization seems to be a displacement of focal 'concern' in a society away from its economic institutions. Displacement from the economic sphere to the political is perhaps most common in contemporary societies where administrative and military issues are inextricably related to politics. It is not that those engaged in political activity place a lower premium upon education than those whose concern is economic productivity (quite the opposite, in many cases), but that the demands imposed upon instruction vary. In times of political crisis, economic and instrumentalist education appears less important than the spreading of a consensus of values, whether to the country at large or to the members of particular groups. Whenever physical confrontation is envisaged or becomes inevitable, instruction will be directed towards military preparation and away from vocational training, as in the case of guerilla corps and/or national mobilization. While the inculcation of qualities of leadership and obedience to

discipline will characterize the education of the armed forces, value-loaded instruction will seek to ensure the solidarity of popular support. Although religious traditionalism has certainly no intrinsic superiority over secular ideology as a source for legitimizing oppsition, it is more likely to be appealed to when (*a*) a 'significant' portion of the population still holds to it (previous policies of secularization having been limited), (*b*) the policies of the secular power have demonstrably denied major tenets of the system of belief (even if this is not the cause of the opposition) and (*c*) the particular religious beliefs and practices are compatible with the secular political goals of the opposition or positively renforce them. India's fight for independence from colonial rule and Israel's fight for survival conform in all points to this pattern.

3. There appear to be certain distinctive characteristics in a religious system which increase the probability that it will be used as a source of legitimation and subsequently incorporated in an institution. Hence the truism that the more a religious form can be associated with cultural and political ends, the more it will tend to be used to further those ends. The common denominator of religions employed in this way can be crudely stated to be a tendency to concentrate upon practice and rites rather than beliefs and emotions, and upon culture rather than conversion. The closer the relationship between religion and national culture, religion being seen as either the 'carrier' (the Polish Catholic Church), the 'raison d'être' (Judaism) or the 'justifier' (Hinduism) of a culture, the lower the resistance of the enlightened to it and to the reintroduction of its symbolic content in education. It is maintained, therefore, that the form a religion takes has an influence upon the possibility of desecularization which is independent of political, economic or intellectual variations. British colonial educational policy in India and West Africa had strikingly different outcomes, considering the degree of similarity in the goals and means employed. In the context of indirect rule, utilitarian instruction sought to produce a native administrative and professional élite of a secular nature. Of the two areas, only India was subject to a policy of acculturation (according to Charles Trevelyan, England was to absorb India as Rome had done Gaul), whereas stricter cultural neutrality was observed in West Africa. Developments at the end of colonial rule reversed expectations, with India reasserting the value of her religious and cultural heritage, while West African education

more readily assimilated the secular value systems oriented to economics. As in many other cases, the character of the indigenous culture proved more important than variations in colonial policy: national religions with long-written traditions, usually hierarchically organized, sometimes with a differentiated body of teachers and with strong ritualistic associations with the indigenous social structure, were more resistant than locally based, relatively undifferentiated religions with oral traditions whose integration with the social structure was restricted to tribe or village level.

3. *The unavoidability of resecularization*

It seems, then, that the complexity of the relationship between religion and the institutional variables that have been discussed precludes deterministic statements which assert the impossibility of desecularization. At the same time, however, Berger's statement that the empirical occurrence of desecularization will be rare has neither been supported nor challenged. In the absence of criteria for frequency, the proposition can be roughly restated in terms of two hypotheses. We have already examined the first: that once a society has been institutionally secularized, religious traditionalism is very unlikely to be reintroduced to give legitimation to authority. The second would state in addition that if institutional desecularization occurred, it would tend to be short-lived. Only theory type C covers this possibility, and it is clear that Berger fully endorses the unavoidability of resecularization:

> Equally interesting is the failure of attempts to replicate the traditional coercive support of religion by the state under conditions of modernization. Contemporary Spain and Israel serve as interesting examples of such attempts, it being safe to say that in both cases the attempts are in the process of failing. We would argue that the only chance of success in these countries would lie in the reversal of the modernization process, which would entail their remaking into pre-industrial societies – a goal as close to the impossible as anything in the realm of history.[22]

Thus resecularization is unavoidable because of the influence of the very factor which accounts for the continuation of secularization itself: the logic of industrialization. While many examples of institutional resecularization can certainly be produced, it remains doubtful whether such shifts in the sources of legitimation are really unavoidable. In other words, it is necessary to show at least one case in which prolonged desecularization did not imply economic decline or stagnation. It would seem that one of the conditions stated as favourable to desecularization, namely extreme political crisis and particularly war, can often further a nation's economic and technical advance at the same time. Other things being equal, and other conditions specified being met, a society legitimated by tradition that was engaged in prolonged defensive or aggressive conflict would not be expected to undergo resecularization. Israel, with its almost complete identification between culture, religion and ethnicity and its history of political conflict, has maintained a high level of economic, technical and educational advance. It could, of course, be argued that a decrease in political tension would favour resecularization, but both elements in the proposition remain at the hypothetical level.

Conclusion

If the optimal conditions for desecularization have been correctly described above, it would appear that each theory type discussed merely highlights a factor unfavourable to the process of desecularization *without precluding it*. It is therefore contended that each theory type has overstressed a trend and overlooked the fact that changes in other variables can influence the control and content of education. The logic of industrialism emphasized the continuous primacy of the economic structure; the logic of rationalism concentrated on the primacy of enlightenment. The dialectical theory, seeking to avoid such materialism or idealism, only succeeds in doing so when discussing the causes of initial secularization: it succumbs to the logic of industrialism when discussing its continuation. Because of this, all three theory types have consistently neglected the religious variable, positing that it is devoid of independent influence and considering the differences in religious institutions and dogmas as irrelevant to modern processes of secularization, desecularization and resecularization.

NOTES

1. 'Toute société qui n'est pas éclairée par les philosophes est trompée par les charlatans.' Condorcet, quoted by J. Bouisso'nnounouse, *Condorcet, le philosoȚ he dasn la Révolution*, Paris 1962, p. 201.

2. J. S. Shapiro, *Condorcet and the Rise of Liberalism*, New York 1934, p. 137.

3. Bryan Wilson, *Religion in Secular Society*, Watts and Co. 1966, p. 58.

4. T. Parsons, 'The School Class as a Social System, Some of its Functions in American Society', *Education, Economy and Society*, ed. A. H. Halsey, J. Floud and C. A. Anderson, Collier-Macmillan 1967, p. 434.

5. M. D. Shipman, *Sociology of the School*, Longmans 1968, p. 9.

6. P. Berger, *The Social Reality of Religion*, Faber and Faber 1969, pp. 110, 127.

7. The theories in this group differ on the exact process of convergence, Condorcet simply positing that as scientists are produced from a non-universal educational system they will increase the national product – which can then be invested in universalizing the system to meet growing demand.

8. P. Berger, op. cit., p. 126.

9. Ibid., p. 131.

10 Ibid., p. 126: 'It is possible to analyse secularization in such a way that it appears a "reflection" of concrete infrastructural processes in modern society.'

11. Ibid. p. 151.

12. Ibid., p. 109.

13. Ibid., p. 129.

14. Ibid., p. 108.

15. Ibid., p. 131.

16. Ibid.

17. J. Kay-Shuttleworth, *Four Periods of English Education*, 1862, pp. 231 f.

18. Napoleon, quoted by E. Rendu, *Monsieur Ambroise Rendu et l'Université de France*, Paris 1861, p. 28: 'Vous croyez que l'homme peut être homme s'il n'a pas Dieu . . . l'homme sans Dieu je l'ai vu à l'oeuvre depuis 1793. Cet homme-là, on ne le gouverne pas, on le mitraille; de cet homme-là j'en ai assez.'

19. G. A. Moumouni, *L'éducation en Afrique*, Paris 1964.

20. Cf. A. Mayhew, *The Education of India*, London 1928.

21. M. de Bauvais, 'Education in former French Africa', *Education and Political Development* ed. J. S. Coleman, Princeton 1965.

22. P. Berger, op. cit., p. 130.

9 The Spiritualist Meeting

Bernice Martin

THE object of this brief study is to describe the main features of the Spiritualist religious service and to suggest that its most appropriate analogues are to be found, not in the religious institutions of modern Christian cultures, but in shamanism, spirit possession and divination. The sequence of discussion will be first a brief outline of the setting – the place, the congregation and the procedure of the service; second, a closer commentary on the three main components of the service – hymns and prayers, the address and the demonstration of clairvoyance; and finally an examination of the ways in which anthropological analyses of shamanism and related phenomena suggest some interpretations of the social nature and significance of this kind of religious experience.

1. *The setting*

The hall in which the Christian Spiritualists meet reminds one more of a warehouse or nissen hut than of an ecclesiastical building. But its damp and slightly peeling plaster is painted bright pink and white, and a small vase of flowers stands before each opaque, barred window. There are perhaps fifty wooden chairs in the body of the hall and a small platform or stage is at the far end. At the back of this stage is a table draped in gold-coloured brocade and holding several more vases of flowers. Above it is a picture of very indifferent artistic merit, though clearly influenced both by William Blake and the pre-Raphaelites. It depicts the Cosmic Being, whose disembodied face and hands hover apparently in an attitude of blessing over the curve of the terrestrial globe against a vivid blue firmament. At the front of the stage are two lecterns, one for the leader of the congregation and one for the visiting medium. Above the front edge of the stage is an alpha/omega sign and, to its left, a hymn board and an inscription of the Seven Principles of the Spiritualists' National Union, printed in gothic lettering, no doubt to reinforce its sacredness:

1. The Fatherhood of God.
2. The Brotherhood of Man.
3. Communion of Spirits and the Ministry of Angels.
4. The Continuous Existence of the Human Soul.
5. Personal Responsibility.
6. Compensation and Retribution hereafter for all the good and evil deeds done on earth.
7. Eternal Progress open to every Human Soul.
   (With Liberty of Interpretation.)

At the Sunday service, which normally takes place in the evening, the congregation usually numbers between twenty and thirty, while a dozen is a good attendance at the mid-week service. The congregation is even more predominantly female and middle-aged than in the Anglican and Nonconformist churches of the town. There are very few family groups with young children, but one notices an occasional atypical family of, say, elderly parents with one quiet daughter of eight or nine. It is not a middle-class congregation but it is not poor either; everyone is neatly if not fashionably dressed. One may sometimes see an obvious unfortunate, a hunchback perhaps, or a woman with a very noticeable hare-lip and nervous twitch, but mostly they are unobtrusive artisans and minor clerks with nothing about them to attract special attention.

There is a nuclear congregation of some fifteen or so people who attend regularly and know each other quite well, though their social contact seems to be confined to the church and seances and does not extend to home visits. Of this group, twos or threes are more closely connected either through kinship (say, mother and daughter or two sisters who come regularly together), or through close friendship (again usually two women of over forty-five). A larger and more diverse group exists on the periphery of the regular congregation. These are intermittent attenders, perhaps regular for a short time and then falling off and returning after weeks or months. Beyond these are the people who come to sample the Spiritualist experience only once or twice, often young girls or adolescent boys who come in little groups and then giggle together in the nearest coffee bar after the service.

The form of the service, though not its content, has been largely taken over from familiar Nonconformist models. The lay leader of the congregation sits on one side of the stage and the visiting medium on the other. The leader begins with a short prayer and introduces the medium; a hymn follows, then a prayer and short address from the medium. Another hymn prefaces the medium's demonstration of clairvoyance, which is the longest item of the service. The congregational leader then reads the notices and introduces the final prayer and hymn, during which a collection is taken.

Cups of tea are offered in the large entrance porch after the service, and the medium and lay leader are available to talk to any member of the congregation who cares to approach them. In my experience, however, only the nuclear congregation normally stays for tea, although anyone else is genuinely welcome. No one attempts to proselytize or press any of the abundant literature from the bookstall on new or intermittent attenders: all positive advances must come from the newcomer if she (or more occasionally he) wants to become integrated into the congregation.

2. *The main components of the service*

The first point to note is the peculiarly attenuated theological content of the Spirtualist system in general, and the consequent theological vagueness of its services. The still, inner, changeless core of the human existence is one with the Cosmic Intelligence; one's spiritual effort is concentrated on realizing this one essential truth. Any other notion of salvation or divine grace is thus denied. Christian Spiritualists are only Christian in seeing Jesus as exemplar, but not as Saviour. Spirits and angels give one psycho-spiritual support, but in the end each individual must realize his own spark of inward divinity. Evil and injustice are not problems, because the endless perfectibility of the human soul both ensures rewards for the good in the hereafter and provides for the less good to be held back, without the harsh intrusion of punitive elements even in the notion of retribution. To paraphrase one medium: 'When we pass over into Spirit we fall naturally to the level of light which we can stand and stay there until our eyes are adjusted to the brightness of the next level.' Though this is clearly an optimistic form of cosmic pantheism it has few detailed or precise dogmas either about the quality of life 'in Spirit' or what constitutes 'the good life' on earth. As the Spiritualist Association puts it, Spiritualism 'confirms much of the thought of the great spiritual leaders of the past, both religious and secular'. One has total freedom of opinion as to what leaders and what aspects of their thought are thus confirmed. 'Goodwill in all personal relationships'[2] and 'the denial of any justification for cruelty'[3] form the core of Spiritualism's social ethic, and while unexceptionable as sentiments they are not always clear, precise or all-embracing as a basis for action. For the most part, however, both in my experience of Spiritualist services and in Spiritualist literature, the main concentration is not on these matters, which might be considered the core of a theology and social ethic, but more narrowly on the notion of human survival after death and the communication of the living with the dead through the work of mediums.

(a) Hymns and prayers

Prayers are a very minor part of the Spiritualist service. They are extempore in Nonconformist fashion, but tend to be short and almost perfunctory. They mostly ask for inspiration and guidance of a very generalized kind from the Cosmic Being. Occasionally they praise Nature. Even more occasionally they refer to political problems, but this is a very insignificant motif.

Hymns are more important. They punctuate the whole service. A few hymns come from Quaker or theologically appropriate Unitarian sources, but many are taken straight from Hymns Ancient and Modern or the Methodist Hymnbook, and the tunes likewise. This extensive borrowing has the very useful function of retaining a sense of familiarity for those who have been brought up within conventional Christianity. The hymns which have been adopted without alteration tend to be those with minimal theological content— simple praise of the Almighty and/or his natural creation: *Awake my soul and with the sun* (Ken), *New every morning is the love* (Keble but unattributed), *Lord of all being throned afar!* (O. W. Holmes), *The spacious firmament on high* (Addison). Other well-known hymns have been cut or rewritten to eliminate references to salvation, atonement, the Sonship of Christ, the struggle against sin, the feebleness of man. *O worship the king* is intact except for the omission of the verse beginning 'Frail children of dust'. The Easter hymn *Jesus lives! Thy terrors now can, O death, no more appal us* becomes

> Loved ones live! No longer now
> Can thy terrors, Death, appal us;
> Angels come! By this we know
> Thou O Grave can'st not enthrall us.

Isaac Watts is extensively used, seldom acknowledged and usually bowdlerized. For instance, *There is a land of pure delight* is almost totally rewritten, altering 'this heavenly land' to 'this Summerland' (a favourite Spiritualist phrase for the world of spirit, though hardly authentic Watts) and eliminating all metaphorical references to Jewish history. *Onward Christian soldiers* reappears as *Onward comrades onward*, complete with martial rhythm and brotherly sentiments.

In addition to the borrowings there are many specially written hymns, without exception of no aesthetic merit whatever. They mostly concern the survival of the soul after death:

> The spirit world has opened wide
> The gates that were 'ajar',
> And loved ones come close by our side
> Whom we had thought afar.
>
> (*Spiritualist Hymnbook* 240)

Some of these hymns specially assert points of difference with Christianity. No. 43, for example, contains the phrase 'No sin-atoning sacrifice can banish pain and woe'. The female principle is more in evidence in the Spiritualist conception of divinity, too. For instance in two hymns chosen at random (41 and 343), God or Spirit is referred to as not only Father but Mother.

There is an undoubted influence of the mid-nineteenth century in the Spiritualist Hymnbook. Its favourite poets (Longfellow, Oliver Wendell Holmes, Harriet Beecher Stowe, Christopher Wordsworth) date from the foundation period of Spiritualism, and the first three remind one of its American origins. Both in these poets and in the persisting choice of imagery in later and inferior imitations, one notes the influence of the nineteenth-century cult of nature, perhaps an offshoot of the romantic movement: 'God speaks to us in bird and song' (64) 'wave-lapped shores', 'melodies of love', 'winged messengers of hope', 'heavenly dew', 'abundant harvest', 'Nature's feast' and so on.

There is too a minor but interesting egalitarian motif in some of the hymns which fits well with a non-élitist theology of ultimate universal perfection, and is highly functional for a group with a predominantly working and lower middle-class congregation. Thus hymn 103 begins:

> All men are brothers, look not down
> On those of humble birth,

> For oft a casket rough contains
> A gem of sterling worth.

(b) The address

The medium's address is seldom longer than ten minutes. It always seems to be delivered spontaneously and without notes. Sometimes the medium goes into a trance and utters the address in the voice and guise of the spirit who possesses him or her. I have, for instance, heard addresses from a mediaeval nun and a first-century Christian martyr. This type of address, however, is remarkably similar in style, length and content to that of a non-possessed medium.

The address is the place, if anywhere, in which one might expect an exposition of the theological and ethical basis of the Spiritualist belief, but this is seldom treated in any depth. The messages of the address are roughly of three kinds: (1) The spirits live and you will live too. (2) Be charitable and full of goodwill and you will have your reward in spiritual fulfilment here and after death. (3) Look inside yourself to your still centre and be content. The modern world is almost invariably depicted as full of harshness, anonymity, superficiality and materialism, and a sociologist might be forgiven for reading into many of these addresses a lament for the passing of *gemeinschaft* – close community and good-neighbourliness. But even if you feel lonely you are not alone because the Cosmic Being is not only with you but inside each and every one. And angels and spirits, 'loved ones from the past' and the like-minded from every time and place, are there to befriend and support even the most forlorn. Violence, anger and open conflict either at a personal or a societal level are seldom discussed and the problems of humanity seem to be primarily conceived of as loneliness, frustration, a sense of being involved only with trivia and a lack of worldly success. Spiritual knowledge will bring patience and cheerfulness in adversity, and a sense of personal achievement more important than what the world regards as success. The metaphors are homely; you will keep cool on the hottest day, you will never get that sinking feeling when the saucepan boils over and the toast burns, and so on. There is often a final peroration on spiritual growth and the life of Spirit, which is full of more abstract metaphors of light and peace.

Some mediums make much of the help one can get from the spirits, while others emphasize the self-sufficiency of the person who understands that the Great First Cause is within every human being.

F

When divinity is both One and Many there is no utltimate contradiction in this. The important point is that there is no concept of human institutions – churches or sacraments – as mediating structures providing grace and confort; the individual and spirit are sufficient. As one medium put it: 'When you need a bit of encouragement, send out a thought to Spirit, but remember, in the end it's up to *you.*'

(c) *The demonstration of clairvoyance*

This is normally the longest item in the service and is clearly the climax for everyone. The medium may occasionally go into a trance or become possessed, but usually it is a much more matter-of-fact procedure. She (or he) will being 'messages from Spirit' to anything between half a dozen and fifteen members of the congregation, pointing to the recipient first, perhaps pausing occasionally to listen to the spirits, perhaps closing her eyes to receive the message, perhaps standing very still, perhaps moving and gesticulating. These demonstrations are fast-moving, colourful and dramatic. Sometimes they are full of wholly-unintended comedy. Mostly they are cosy rather than awesome.

Each medium has his or her personal brand of clairvoyance, her recognizable range of phrase, mannerism and imagery. Some specialize, as it were, in spirit guides, some in dead relatives and friends, some in colourful objects of undefined but rich symbolic significance such as golden trumpets and rainbow auras. Some receive verbal messages from spirits, some just a feeling or even a smell, the significance of which they try to convey in words: 'There's a grcat feeling of warmth and love here, like a family round a warm hearth.' For some mediums the spirits almost always bring pets, and even wild animals: 'You see, our four-legged friends live too, dear.' For some, they bring objects of domestic significance such as a pipe or a favourite chair. Several women mediums have a complex and well-developed code of meanings in the flowers which the spirits so often 'present' to their living kin.

There is no doubt that most mediums are very sensitive to the social and personal situation of the members of the congregation. Although they are a peripatetic profession, their circuit brings them back to the same churches many times. They undoubtedly get to know the regular congregation quite well; they learn their family histories, likes and needs both in the social sessions after the service and in the course of several demonstrations of clairvoyance. They remember that Mrs A. had a husband called George of this or that personal and physical type, that she has two favourite spirit guides of such and such description, and so on. They must also know from experience that only certain categories of persons tend to come to Spiritualist services, in particular the ageing, the lonely and the bereaved. With practice one is able, even without being aware that one is doing it, to pick up the clues which most people so generously offer in their appearance, demeanour and verbal responses to the medium when she begins to transmit the messages.

Where the recipient is new or unknown the first messages tend to be very ambiguous until from the recipient's responses a fruitful line of development is revealed. 'I see a question mark, a big one. Could that mean you have a problem, dear?' 'Yes, lots.' 'Have you been feeling low or depressed recently – I have a feeling like a great weight on my back.' The exact nature of the problem is seldom communicated except with the regular congregation whose ailments or family problems are sometimes referred to a little more explicitly. With youngish people the 'problem' approach is often the first to be tried. If they own no material problem there are always unrecognized spiritual ones. Quite often too the medium senses a bereavement. 'Would I be right in thinking that father is in Spirit?' 'No, mother's dead.' 'Yes, I could feel a close relative in Spirit but mother hasn't shown herself yet. The spirits take their own time, dear.' Mother normally does show herself quite soon and sends messages of love and understanding.

Quite frequently names are offered, usually of the generation which will most recently have 'gone to Spirit' – Ada, Fred, Maggie, Albert. If the name has no significance for the recipient he or she is asked to check family records or told that it might have been a friend of grandfather's. Sometimes a figure is described: 'I have a gentleman here in a slightly old-fashioned suit, a little thick in the body with hair greying at the temples. Does that mean anything to you?' Or 'I have someone here who tells me he was a bit heavy with the salt and pepper. Would that be anyone you know?' 'I don't think so.' 'Then perhaps you are a little heavy-handed with something that you should take more easy.'

It is very seldom indeed that no bell is rung by these messages and the false notes are very quickly passed over with 'Never mind dear, perhaps it will suggest something to you if you think about it.' Since everything can be taken either literally or metaphorically, something always will suggest itself with a little effort. Most of the spirit messages are notable too for the triviality of their content. Often they are little more than indeterminate domestic references. 'There's some kind of joke here. The spirits are laughing about rhubarb.' 'Well, we did have an allotment.' One medium explained that though this kind of thing may seem trivial, the important thing was that the spirits were showing their 'trademarks' 'or finger-prints' to their loved ones on earth: it was a demonstration of per-sonal survival and so gave comfort and hope. The messages clearly do have this function, and often something more. Once a spirit is identified he or she sends messages of love, comfort, understanding, protec-tion: 'And they say take care of your poor legs in the cold weather.' Happy kinship and friendship ties are renewed and conflicts with the dead can be resolved. 'Father was very stiff, even domineering, wasn't he? Well, he has grown in Spirit. He understands now.' 'Mother didn't always see your point of view on earth, did she dear? Well, she understands now.' Guilt, frustration, a sense of rejection or iso-lation, can all be alleviated by the clairvoyance process. It is more important to be forgiven by my father in Spirit than Our Father in Heaven.

The second major social function of the clairvoyance seems to be to reinforce the recipient's identification with his allotted social role and give him a sense of purpose to carry on in what must often be a colourless existence. The message is 'Accept accept! Make the best of what you have, be cheerful and thankful and concentrate on spiri-tual development.' In theory the medium could easily adopt a prophe-tic role and preach a millenial message of revolt, but this does not happen and would provoke little response in most Spiritualist con-gregations if it did. Nor does one find examples such as Malcolm Calley[4] noted among West Indian Pentecostalists of the religious leader using his role in the service to strengthen his hand against a rival faction in the congregation. Quite the contrary. I have witnessed several occasions on which the medium has used his or her position as a relative outsider to resolve tensions within the congregation by explaining in Spirit messages that X has been irritable, or the organist has been missing services because he has special problems, is under mental and spiritual stress and so forth. Spiritualism functions to reinforce and not to undermine the social order by relieving stresses and enabling individuals to play out their social roles even in trying circumstances.

The colour, drama and quiet excitement of the clairvoyance sessions is an important constituent of this reinforcing social therapy. There is minimal visual satisfaction – no ritual and few aesthetic trappings – but the verbal skill of the mediums is often considerable. They describe colours and shapes vividly and with noticeable pleasure both to themselves and the congregation. The Spirit Guides are important here too. It seems initially curious that these guides should consist quite disproportionately of Chinese Mandarins, Aztecs, Hindu gurus, Red Indians (one thinks again of Longfellow) and sweet-faced mediaeval nuns – the only female guides of any significance. But these are not only romantic figures, they are associated in the popular imagination with ancestor cults of various kinds, and even nuns are thought to see and become ghosts more often than ordinary European mortals. Moreover, their faces and costumes lend themselves to virtuoso passages of description. Some people must come to feel that they know their spirit guides very well as they gradually reveal dramatic or curious items from their own past history. The insignificance of one's daily routine can be transfigured by the conviction that a powerful and romantic spirit guide is always beside you. For some people the same kind of ego-reinforcement can come from having spiritual converse with the famous dead in the clairvoyance demonstrations or more likely in private seances. Either way Spiritualism can be a powerful source of comfort and confidence to its adherents.

3. *Discussion*

If one were trying to categorize Spiritualism on a church/sect spectrum the most appropriate category seems to be what has been variously called the cult (Becker, Martin) or the Gnostic sect (Wilson). But the distance of Spiritualism from the Judeo-Christian tradition for which these conventional categories were specifically developed makes the exercise ultimately unprofitable, as the anonymous reviewer of G. K. Nelson's book on Spiritualism[5] pointed out (*Times Literary Supplement*, 26 June 1969). In fact the most appropriate anologues of modern Spiritualism are shamanism, spirit mediumship and divination in small-scale societies, and in some historic cultures such as classical Greece and Rome. The parallel with classical religions cannot here be pursued, but anthropological analyses of these phenomena can be applied with very little modification to Spiritualism and can in turn suggest further aspects of the cult which might be fruitfully studied.

One of the most succinct and cogent discussions of the anthropological findings is Victor Turner's article on Religious Specialists in the new *Encyclopaedia of the Social Sciences*.[6] Anthropologists seem to have had less use for Max Weber's concepts and categories in the sociology of religion than for Durkheim's much-abused distinction between priest and medicine man: on the one hand the ritual leader of communal religious practices which directly affirm and reinforce the social entity, and on the other the private practitioner who offers his thaumaturgical services to all comers. Turner develops this into a distinction between the institutional functionary (the priest) and the inspirational functionary. Prominent in the latter category are the shaman and the spirit medium, respectively the active and passive vessels of spirit possession. Perhaps the most economical way of indicating the striking similarities between Spiritualism and its anthropological analogues is to set out in a table the major distinguishing features of priests on the one hand, and shamans and spirit mediums on the other, with a third column showing the aspects of Spiritualism which resemble the second category. A second table will similarly indicate the differences between prophet and shaman since, though both are 'inspirational' functionaries their social characteristics are very dissimilar. I shall draw heavily on Turner's analysis in doing this.

Divination – which in Turner's phrase is the attainment of knowledge of secret or future things by methods other than the rational procedures of natural science – is an art which may be practised by priest and prophet, although usually with reference to communal rather than individual needs. But it is peculiarly characteristic of the shaman and medium. Turner's own detailed study of shamanistic divination among the Ndembu[7] shows a process very closely paralleling the demonstrations of clairvoyance outlined above and some aspects of the Spiritualist healing service which there is not space to describe here: the shaman's sensitivity to clues about the client's personal identity and problems, his implicit and sometimes even overt analysis of the client's social context, and so on. The diviner's ultimate function, so Turner argues, is to reintegrate social groups, usually small in scale, which have been threatened with disruption

Priest	Shaman and Spirit Medium	Spiritualism
1 Powers inherited or acquired by training	Powers 'by divine stroke' – often through personal communication from a supernatural being. Sometimes supplemented by training.	Mediums 'called' by experience of contacting spirits or being sensitive to psychic phenomena.
2 Institutional function rites for whole community.	Private or semi-private function. Most frequently operates for individual clients and their kin group.	Mediums not leaders of congregation but a peripatetic profession functioning in services (as described above) and in healing services, small group seances and private consultations.
3 Rites often calendrical.	Rites rarely calendrical: usually curative and contingent upon occasions of mishap or illness.	No liturgical calendar, only natural seasons marked and Easter (i.e. Resurrection, seeing Jesus as merely the type case, but not Passion, or Incarnation); otherwise regularly available curative rites, especially healing services.
4 Symbolic forms of rite predominantly involve sensory objects with traditional significance for whole community-bread, chalice, etc., i.e., priest manipulates objects.	Symbolic forms not predominantly sensory objects but verbalizations of what is in the mind of the possessed shaman, etc., i.e. shaman describes his vision	Minimal visual ritual. Aesthetic and symbolic content of service predominantly in the medium's speech.
5 Maintains and re-inforces tradition and coherence of whole social group.	Less concern for total cultural system; more sensitive to the personal, private, mutable, idiosyncratic.	Clear concern for and sensitivity to the personal and small-scale rather than large-scale societal issues.

Prophet	Shaman and Spirit Medium	Spiritualism
1 Like priest tends to deal direct with major divinities on behalf of whole community.	Deals with minor spirits for narrower and more immediate purposes.	Divinity and even angels much less prominent than spirits of the dead, usually the fairly recently dead.
2 Often a radical reformer or revolutionary leader. Sees self as *outside* conventional social structure.	Not a radical or revolutionary leader. Essentially part of the social structure whose members he services.	Spiritualist mediums indirectly underpin rather than undermine the social structure.

by the inability of one or more members to accept or play out their allotted social roles. Thus the treatment of individuals or small groups is important for the smooth functioning of a wider social structure.

The shaman often acts as guardian of social harmony in another way too. In some societies which lack autonomous political authority separate from the kin organization, the shaman may take on a para-political role in reconciling conflicting kin groups after a homicide or in a feud situation. He is able to perform this delicate function, not because he is powerful, but precisely because as a *private* magico-religious specialist he is partly outside the structured hierarchy of the society. In a very minor way the occasional role of the Spiritualist medium in relieving inter-congregational strains and hostilities is not dissimilar.

Spiritualism, however, differs from shamanism and spirit medium-ship in small-scale societies in a few interesting respects. It is in theory a self-sufficient religious institution, not a mere supplement to priestly religion. Yet a significant minority of at least the peripheral congregation are also residual adherents of a conventional church or denomination, and there is nothing in the Spiritualist movement which even discourages this.

A second point of difference is that in modern Spiritualism there is little trace of that fear of the dead which often characterizes shamanism in small-scale societies, and indeed marks popular attitudes to ghosts in our own society. Far from being maliciously demanding of their living kin, the dead seem to be regarded as uniformly benevolent. Moreover, spiritualist divination is not normally employed to expose or punish those responsible for social or psychological distress. The conflicts which Spiritualism heals are seldom openly acknowledged, whereas in many small-scale societies the process of divination and the work of the shaman function precisely to give open expression, often at inordinate length, to inter-group resentments, conflicts and tensions before harmony can be achieved.

The most important parallels with modern Spiritualism here are in China and Japan, where ancestors are also predominantly regarded as benevolent. Maurice Freedman[8] has argued persuasively that the contrast between these ancient civilizations and most other cases of ancestor-worship rests on two interconnected factors: first the scale of the society and second the mode of perception and explanation. In small-scale societies, evil and misfortune are experienced as embedded in personal relationships and are therefore explained in personalized terms: hence the fear of the dead. By contrast, in the more complex societies of Japan and China the mode of explanation is predominantly impersonal and evil is accordingly attributed to more remote and abstract causes: hence the benignity of ancestors. It was noted above that modern society as such was seen as the impersonal source of frustration and misfortune in many Spiritualist prayers and addresses, whereas happiness and fulfilment came from inward personal experience and face-to-face relationships. Freedman further argues that the nature of ancestor worship in China and Japan cannot be understood except through an analysis of the whole role structure of the family, and especially the transmission of authority. The notion of the benignity of the ancestors is strong enough to inhibit the expression of intra-familial conflict but not strong enough to eliminate it completely. The incumbents of ambiguous roles within the family structure may either degrade the ancestors by manipulating them for personal gain (through feng-shui) or perceive and treat them as potentially hostile: married women in particular seem likely to do the latter. This again is a clue well worth pursuing in relation to modern Spiritualism. A fuller study of spirit message and the process of spiritualist healing might reveal a great deal about the sources of tension and role conflict in the modern family.

Just as overt reference to aggression and fear is toned down in modern Spiritualism, so are extravagant physical signs of spirit possession. Devices such as ventriloquism, sleight of hand, drumming dancing and other aids to putting medium and audience into a trance-like state have often been regarded as inseparable from shamanism because they were found in classical examples such as the Siberian Chuckchee. But studies such as Nadel's among the Nuba[9] have shown that shamanism in some simple societies lacks these trappings too. It would be interesting to explore the factors which might account for the presence or absence of such phenomena.

Another point worth further exploration is the suggestion found in some anthropological texts that shamans are differentially recruited from the neurotic (Nadel).[10] the 'neuropath' and those with negative external qualities such as ugliness or weakness (Eliade)[11] or the socially or psychologically 'marginal' (Turner).[12] It has further been suggested that shamans may be more 'pathological' in all these ways than more passive mediums (Morris).[13] This is in part the recurrent and unanswered problem of whether all religious virtuosi and/or charismatic leaders are or are not personally pathological. It is perhaps also another way of approaching the point made above that the private practitioner as distinct from the institutional religious functionary has in some sense a marginal or 'interstitial' role in the society. This may sometimes be expressed in the shaman's personal characteristics but it can as easily be a *structured* marginality, as it is for example among the Nuer where the so-called 'leopard-skin priest' (shaman) is part of a small lineage among more powerful kin groups whose status he can never threaten. There is no evidence as to whether Spiritualist mediums are more pathological than the rest of the population, but it would be unwise to dismiss the issue without looking a little further at the possibility of 'marginality'. At least two mediums in the course of their addresses made direct reference to their own experiences of marginality – the lonely, unloved boy in the Anglican rectory and the frustrated secretary ticking over in a status and occupation below her capacities until she discovered her psychic powers. The latter example, especially in view of the dominance of women among Spiritualist mediums, leads to speculation in another direction too. Could it be that becoming a medium is functionally equivalent to entering, say, social work or other 'expressive' feminine professions for some women whose educational background and social horizons makes these secular professions an unrealistic objective? The suggestion might be more fruitful than the search for 'pathological' personality types among mediums.

A final point which the anthropological literature raises is the nature of the kin and community structures in which Spiritualists are involved. In tribal societies shamanism is predominantly found in small, multi-functional, loosely bonded communities. This might well prove a more interesting line of exploration in any future studies of the background of Spiritualists than the usual preoccupation with social class alone is likely to afford.

NOTES

1. The Spiritualist Association of Great Britain. This and the two quotations which follow are part of the account of Spiritualism's aims and achievements stated inside the front cover of every edition of *The Spiritualist*, published monthly.
2. See above.
3. See above.
4. M. J. C. Calley, *God's People*, OUP 1965.

5. G. K. Nelson, *Spiritualism and Society*, Routledge and Kegan Paul 1969. See also G. K. Nelson, 'The Spiritualist Movement: A need for the redefinition of the concept of Cult', *Journal for the Scientific Study of Religion*, Spring 1969, Vol. XIII, No. 1, p. 152.

6. E. R. A. Seligman (ed.), *Encyclopedia of the Social Sciences*, Collier-Macmillan 1937, Vol. B, p. 437.

7. See V. Turner, *Ndembu Divination: Its Symbolism and Techniques*, Manchester University Press 1961 and V. Turner, *The Forest of Symbols*, OUP 1969.

8. M. Freedman, 'Ancestor Worship: Two Facets of the Chinese Case', *Social Organisation* ed. M. Freedman, Cass and Co. 1967.

9. S. F. Nadel, 'Studies of Shamanism in the Nuba Mountains', *Reader in Comparative Religion*, ed. E. Z. Vogt and W. A. Lessa, Harper and Row, 1965.

10. Nadel, art cit.

11. M. Eliade, *Patterns in Comparative Religion*, Sheed and Ward 1958. p. 18.

12. V. Turner, *The Forest of Symbols*, esp. ch. 6.

13. H. S. Morris, 'Shamanism among the Oya Melanau', *Social Organisation* ed. M. Freedman, Cass and Co. 1967.

10 Bibliography of Work in the Sociology of British Religion,* July 1969

Robert W. Coles

THIS bibliography is part of a larger bibliography, prepared as part of the social analysis of religion project at the Institute of Social and Economic Research, University of York. It does not include items which were listed in the bibliography prepared by David Martin and published in *A Sociology of English Religion*, SCM Press 1967.

The main focus of the bibliography is on the contemporary religious situation. Factual material, however, must be understood against the background of its historical development, especially when trying to understand the processes of which the contemporary situation is just a part. In collecting material, however, some arbitrary dateline had to be drawn. This has been 1851, the year of the first, and only, census of religious worship in Britain. The dateline has not been rigidly adhered to, and material which provides a background to the mid-nineteenth century when the census was carried out, has been included. To cover over a century of socio-religious development as well would have been too great a task. Only a selection of historical material is therefore included.

It is also notoriously difficult to distinguish between sociology and non-sociology, and the attempt may well have excluded on technical grounds, which themselves may be disputed, many entries which provide rich source material to the professional sociologist. Many works by psychologists have been included, since it seems important to the author that sociological theories be consonant with psychological theories. Again in the study of social processes, the psychological mechanisms seem as important to a full discussion as their historical context. Psychological works have, however, only been

* The author wishes to acknowledge help given by Dr David Martin, Dr Colin Campbell and Mr Louis Billington in the collection of material for this bibliography.

included where they have a direct bearing on the understanding of the empirical situation under examination.

1. *General Surveys and Comments on Religion and Society*

Allcock, J. B., 'Voluntary Association and the Structure of Power', *Sociological Review*, Vol. 16 (1), 1969

Banks, J. A., 'The Sociology of Religion in England', Sociologische Gids, January 1963 10 (I)

Barritt, D. P. & Carter, C. F., *The Northern Ireland Problem*, OUP 1962

Bedouelle, G., *L'Église d'Angleterre et la Société Politique Contemporaine*, Librarie Générale de Droit et de Jurisprudence, 1968

Brothers, J. B., *Report of 4th Consultation of the European Colloquium on the Sociology of Religion*, William Temple College

Brothers, J. B., 'Youth and a changing church', *New Life*, 1964

Buchanan, 'Religion and the Working Class', *Theology* 61, May 1958

Byrnes J. P. K., 'A Study of the Differences between Anglicans and Methodists' Churches on such questions as drink and gambling', *Anglican–Methodist Relations* ed. W. S. F. Pickering, Darton, Longman & Todd 1961

Callard, Mary P., 'The Church and older people', *Social Service Quarterly*, Vol. 33 (3), 1959

Carter, M. P., 'Report on a Survey of Research in Britain', *Sociological Review* 16 (1), March 1968

Church of England Youth Council, 'Training Christians', unpublished paper

Church of England Youth Council, 'Training in Action', unpublished paper

Currie, R., *Methodism Divided*, Faber & Faber 1968

Driberg, T., 'Pragmatic Piety – The Church of England in the 20th Century' *Texas Quarterly Review*, pp. 63–75, 1960

Duffield, G. E. (ed.), *The Paul Report considered*, Abingdon, The Marcham Manor Press 1964

Hammersley, J., 'Christians and the world', *New Society*, 24 August 1967

Hill, M., 'Modern Religion in Search of Meaning' (review article) *Times Educational Supplement*, 18 April 1969

Hodgkins, W., *Sunday, Christian and social significance*, Independent Press 1960

Irving, G., 'A Sociology of High and Low', *Faith and Unity*, November 1966

Jones, K. S., 'An enquiry into some aspects of religion in relation to psychiatry', *Sociological Review*, Vol. 17 (1), 1969

Krausz, E., *Sociology in Britain*, Batsford 1969

Krausz, E., 'Religion as a Key Variable', unpublished article (City University)

Lloyd, R., *The Church of England 1900–1965*, SCM Press 1966

Loudon, J. B., 'Religious order and mental disorder', *British Journal of Preventive and Social Medicine*, 16, 1962

MacInnes, C., 'A Godless Nation', *New Society*, 29 August 1963

MacIntyre A., 'Marxists and Christians', *Twentieth Century*, Autumn 1961, pp. 28–38

MacIntyre, A., *Secularization and Moral Change*, OUP 1967

MacIntyre, A., 'The Christian–Communist Rapprochement: Some Sociological Notes and Questions', *A Sociological Yearbook of Religion in Britain*, ed. D. A. Martin, SCM Press 1969

MacWorth, J., 'Religion and the Mentally Sick: some fundamental issues', *Religion and Mental Health*, National Association for Mental Health, London 1960

Martin, D. A., 'The Sociology of religion: a case of status deprivation', *British Journal of Sociology*, 14 (4). December, 1966

Martin, D. A., *The Religious and the Secular*, Routledge & Kegan Paul 1969

Martin, D. A., 'The Unknown Gods of the English', *Advancement of Science*, June 1966

Mason, D. H. and Roberts, W. J., 'Methodism in Wales 1950–60', A confidential report

Matchet, F., 'Religion on the Air', *New Society*, 4 March 1965

Mayfield, G., *The Church of England: its members and business*, OUP, 2nd edition 1963

Mayor, S. H., 'The Religion of the British People', *Hibbert Journal*, 59, October 1960

Mercer, A. & Shepherd, A. J., 'Operational Research – the Church of England', unpublished paper, Dept. of Operational Research, University of Lancaster 1969

Mercer, A., O'Neil, J. S. & Shepherd, A. J., *The Churching of Urban England: an unknown report*, unpublished, University of Lancaster

Miagret, M., *The National Church and the social order*, Church of England Information Board 1956

Moore, R. S., 'Religion and Immigration in an urban twilight zone', *Advancement of Science*, Vol. 23, June 1966

National Association of Mental Health, *The Role of Religion in Mental Health*, 1966

O'Brien, C. Cruise, 'Holy War in Ireland', *New York Review of Books*, Vol. XIII, no. 8, 6 Nov. 1969

O'Donovan, P., 'Catholicism and Class', *Twentieth Century*, Spring 1965 pp. 52–57

Opum, M., 'Sex differences in sin preferences', *Psychological Reports* 21 (3), 1967, pp. 752–67

Peel, J., 'Birth Control and Catholic Doctrine', *London Quarterly and Holborn Review*, October 1965

Pickering, W. S. F., 'Established Churches and the Community', *London Quarterly and Holborn Review*, April 1963

Roberts, F. J., 'Some Psychological factors in religious conversion', *British Journal of Social and Clinical Psychology*, Vol. 4 (3) 1965

Robertson, D. R., 'The relationship of Church and Class in Scotland', *A Sociological Yearbook of Religion in Britain I*, ed. D. A. Martin, SCM Press 1968

Rodd, C., 'Denominational Values', *Sociology*, Vol. 2 (i), January 1968

Salter, N., *Christians and the Common Market*, SCM Press 1967

Simey, T., 'The Church of England and English Society', *Social Compass*, Vol. II (3), 1964, pp. 5–19,

Sinclair, J., *The Effects of some ideological factors in Voluntary Youth Movements: a study of the Scout Movement*, M.A., Edinburgh 1967

Smith, J. W. D., *Psychology and religion in early childhood*, SCM Press 1963

Spencer, A. E. C. W., 'Social Class and religious behaviour in England', *Clergy Review*, January 1968

Spencer, A. E. C. W., 'Youth and Religion: religious attitudes, beliefs and practices of Urban Youth', *New Life*, 14 (1), 1958

Thompson, K., 'Bureaucracy and the Church' *A Sociological Yearbook of Religion in Britain*, ed. D. A. Martin, SCM Press 1968

Viney, M., 'The Five Percent', *Irish Times*, 22–26 March 1965

Ward, C. K., 'Socio-research in the sphere of religion in Britain', *Sociologia religiosa* (3–4), 1959, pp. 79–94

Ward, C. K., 'Socio-religious research in Ireland', *Social Compass*, Vol. II (3) 1964, pp. 25–29

William Temple College, Rugby, *Mainstream religion: a study of the content of religious broadcasting during June 1963*, June 1963

Wilson, B. R., 'Establishment, Sectarianism and partisanship', *Sociological Review* 15 (2), July 1967

Wilson, B. R., 'God in Retirement', *Twentieth Century*, 170 (1011), Autumn 1961

2. *Historical Background* (*selection*)

Bowen, D., *The Idea of the Victorian Church: A Study of the Church of England 1833–89*, Montreal, McGill 1968

Budd, S., 'Loss of Faith in England 1850–1950', *Past and Present* No. 36, London 1967

Butler, Violet, *Social Conditions in Oxford*, Sidgwick & Jackson 1912

Cairns, D. A. (ed.), *The Army and Religion*, 1919

Chadwick, O., *The Mind of the Oxford Movement*, A & C Black 1960

Currie, R., 'The Anglican Prayer Book Controversy – power and principle', *Church History*, June 1964, p. 192

Deane, A. C., 'The Falling off in the quantity and quality of the clergy', *Nineteenth Century*, 45 268, pp. 1023–30

Durant, Ruth, *Watling: A survey of social life on a new housing estate*, London, P. S. Kind & Sons 1930

Elliot Binns, L. E., *The Early evangelicals – a religious and social study*, Lutterworth Press 1953

Glaser, J. F., *Nonconformity and Liberalism 1865-1885*, unpublished, PhD Harvard 1948

Goodridge, R. M., 'The Religious Condition of the West Country in 1851', *Social Compass* 14 (4), 1967

Goodridge, R. M., 'Nineteenth-century Urbanization and Religion: Bristol and Marseilles, 1830-1880', *A Sociological Yearbook of Religion in Britain 2*, ed. D. A. Martin, SCM Press, 1969

Gowland, D. A., 'Rochdale Politics and Methodist Schism', *Wesley Historical Society, Lancashire and Cheshire Branch Occasional Publications* 1965

Hammond, E. G., *Farm servants, and agricultural labourers: their moral and religious condition*, London 1856

Hawkins, C. B., *Norwich: a social survey*, London, Philip Lee Warner 1910

Heasman, Kathlean, *Evangelicals in Action*, Geoffrey Bles 1962

Horner, Rev. J., *The Influence of Methodism on the Social Structure and Culture of rural Northumberland from 1820-1914*, M.A. thesis in progress, University of Newcastle

Hume, Rev. A., *Conditions of Liverpool, religious and social, with notices of the state of education, morals, pauperism and crime*, London 1868

Hume, Rev. A., *Missions at Home, or a clergyman's account of a portion of the town of Liverpool*, London 1850

Israel, H., 'Some religious factors in the emergence of industrial society in England', *American Sociological Review* 31 (5), October 1966

Journeyman Engineer, *Some Habits and Customs of the Working Classes*, London 1867

Liverpool Argus, 'The Churches in Liverpool', 1878

Liverpool Daily Post, 'Religious censuses decennially from 1831 to 1912', 13 December 1912

Loosley, E. G., 'Membership Statistics – The first decade of the Twentieth Century', *Methodist Recorder*, 7 July 1910

Loosley, E. G., 'The Census and Methodist Membership – A ten year comparison of returns', *Methodist Recorder*, 8 September 1921

Loosley, E. G., 'The Census and Methodist Membership – Abreast an Increasing Population', *Methodist Recorder*, 16 July 1931

Lynd, H., *England in the Eighteen Eighties*, OUP 1947

Mason, B. J., *The Rise of Combative Dissent 1832-1859*, unpublished M.A. thesis, University of Southampton

Maurice-Davies, C., *Mystic London*, London 1875

Maurice-Davies, C., *Unorthodox London*, London 1874

Maurice-Davies, C., *Orthodox London*, London 1874

Mayor, S. H., *The Churches and the Labour Movement*, Independent Press 1967

Mess, H. A., *Industrial Tyneside*, Ernest Benn 1928

Miall, E., *The British Churches in Relation to the British People*, London 1859

Mudie-Smith, P., *The Religious Life of London*, Hodder & Stoughton 1904

Nottingham Daily Express, 'Religious Census of the City of Nottingham', 8 Dec. 1881

Pickering, W. S. F., 'The 1851 census: a useless experiment', *British Journal of Sociology* 1967

Roberts, D. A., *The Orange Movement in Ireland 1886–1916*, OUP 1970

Rowntree, B. S., *Poverty: a study of town life*, Longmans 1901

Rowntree, B. S., *Poverty and Progress*, Longmans 1941

Sandhurst, B. G., *How Heathen is Britain?*, London 1946

Sellers, I., 'Nonconformist Attitudes in Late Nineteenth-century Liverpool', *Transactions of the Historical Society of Lancashire and Cheshire*, Vol. 114, 1962

Spinks, G. S., *Religion in Britain since 1900*, Andrew Dakers 1952

Taylor, E. R., *Methodism and Politics, 1791–1851*, CUP 1935

Tillyard, E. H., 'Distribution of Free Churches in England', *Sociological Review* 27, 1935

Vincent, J. R., *Poll books – How Victorians Voted*, CUP 1966

Wearmouth, R. F., *Methodism and working class movements in England, 1800–1850*, Epworth Press 1947

Wearmouth, R. F., *Methodism and the struggle of the Working Classes 1850–1900*, Leicester, Edgar Backins 1954

Wearmouth, R. F., *The Social and Political Influences of Methodism in the Twentieth Century*, Epworth Press 1957

3. *Statistical Material*

Butler, J. & Jones, B., 'Statistical Analysis of Membership of the Methodist Church', unpublished paper, University of Kent, Canterbury

Campbell, C. B., 'Membership composition of the British Humanist Association', *Sociological Review*, Vol. 3 (3), November 1965, pp. 327–337

Catholic Education Council, *Catholic Education. A Handbook*, 1962

Central Board of Finance of the Church of England, *Facts and Figures about the Church of England*. No. 3, Church Information Office 1965

Chou, R. C. and Brown S., 'A comparison of the size of families of Roman Catholics and non Roman Catholics in Great Britain', *Population Studies*, Vol. 22 (1), March 1968

Economist, 'How many in the pew?' *Economist*, 30 August 1958

Free Church Federal Council, *Yearbooks*

Gay, J., 'Distribution of Catholics and Mormons', *A Sociological Yearbook of Religion in Britain 1*, ed. D. A. Martin, SCM Press 1968

Highet, J., 'Churchgoing in Scotland', *New Society*, 26 December 1963

Jones, B. E., 'Manchester Study of lapsed members – Ministers Views', unpublished 1962[1]

Jones, B. E., 'Sheffield Study of lapsed members – Ministers Views', unpublished 1962[1]

Jones, B. E., 'Lapsed members. London S.W.', unpublished 1963[1]

Jones, B. E., 'Study of lapsed members, Nottingham', unpublished 1964[1]

Jones, B. E., 'Manchester Membership Survey', unpublished 1964–65[1]

Pickering, W. S. F., 'The Present position of the Anglican and Methodist Churches in the light of available statistics', *Anglican–Methodist Relations*, ed. W. S. F. Pickering, Darton, Longman & Todd 1961

Spencer, A. E. C. W., 'Notes Towards the statistical definition of the Church', *International Conference on Religious Sociology*, Konigstein 1962

Spencer, A. E. C. W., 'The Newman Demographic Survey 1953–64. Reflections on the birth, life and death of a Catholic institute of socio-religious research', *Social Compass* II (3), 1964

Spencer, A. E. C. W., 'The Demography and sociography of the Catholic Community in England and Wales', *Downside Symposium*, reprinted in *The Committed Church*, ed. Bright and Clements, Darton, Longman & Todd 1965

Spencer, A. E. C. W., 'Report on the Parish register statistics of the Roman Catholic Church in Scotland 1966', Harrow Middlesex, Pastoral Research Centre, 1967

[1] Available from Wesley College, Bristol

4. *Community and Parish Studies*

Bazire, Rev. R. V., Battersea Deanery Survey, May 1965

Bell, C., 'Findings', *New Society*, 30 May 1968

Bell, C. & Batstone, E., 'Banbury Social Survey', Research in Progress, U. C. Swansea

Bird, A. H., Summary of replies to questionnaires distributed to Working Men's Clubs, Public Houses, Bingo Halls, etc., *Free Church Chronicle*, April 1966

Bleakley, D., *Young Sister and Religion in the Sixties*, Church of Ireland Group, 80 North Rd., Belfast 4, 1964

Bracey, H. E., *Neighbours: on new estates and sub-divisions in England and USA*, Routledge & Kegan Paul 1964

Brett, H., 'Methodism and Racial Differences', *Methodist Recorder*, 13 October 1921

Broady, M., *Survey of Religious Behaviour and Attitudes in Southampton*, unpublished survey, Southampton University 1968

Carr-Saunder, A. M., Caradog Jones & Moser, *A Survey of Social Conditions in England and Wales*, Clarendon Press 1958

Davis, *The Parish and the modern world*, Sheed & Ward 1965

Dennis, N., Henriques & Slaughter, *Coal is our Life*, Eyre & Spottiswoode 1956

Dodds, P., 'Who goes to Church?', *New Society*, 29 April 1965

Droylesden and Hampstead Circuit, 'Survey of Attendance on one Sunday night', unpublished 1966[1]

Goy, L. R., 'Kilburn and Hampstead Circuit – an analysis of Membership, unpublished 1967[1]

Hill, M. and Wakeford, P., 'Disembodied Ecumenicalism. A Survey of members of four Methodist Churches in or near London', *A Sociological Yearbook of Religion in Britain 2*, ed. D. A. Martin SCM Press 1969

Hill, M. & Turner, B. R., 'The Laity and Church Unity', *New Christian*, 17 April 1969

Hinings, C. R., 'The Balsall Heath Survey: a report', *Research Bulletin*, Univ. of Birmingham, Institute for the study of religious worship and architecture, 1967

Hinings, C. R., 'The Hodge Hill Survey', *Research Bulletin*, Univ. of Birmingham, Institute for the study of religious worship and architecture, 1966

Hudson, K., *An Awkward Size for a Town* [Swindon] David & Charles, 1967

Jackson, M. J. & Mann, P. H., 'Anglican-Methodist Relations in Two Urban Parishes', *Anglican-Methodist Relations*, ed. W. S. F. Pickering, Darton, Longman & Todd 1961

Jackson, M. J., 'Major issues in industrial missions', *International Review of Missions*, 54 (215) April 1965

Jennings, Hilda, *Societies in the Making*, Routledge & Kegan Paul 1962

Kaim-Caundle, P. R., 'Religion in Billingham 1957–1959', Billingham Community Association

Kaim-Caundle, P. R., 'Church and social change: a study of religion in Billingham 1959–66', *New Christian*, 9 March 1967

New England (Peterborough), Report of Enquiry, May 1965[1]

Portwood, D., 'The moulding of a City and its churches: Stoke on Trent, Paper prepared for the Sociology Dept., Keele

Pagden, F. T., 'An analysis of the effectiveness of Methodist Churches of varying types and sizes in the Liverpool district', *A Sociological Yearbook of Religion in Britain 1*, ed. D. A. Martin, SCM Press, 1968

Rex, J. & Moore, R., *Race Community and Conflict*, OUP, 1967

Smart, M., 'The Local Unit of the future church', *New Directions*, Summer 1967

Spencer, A. E. C. W., 'Religious Census of Bishop Stortford', *A Sociological Yearbook of Religion in Britain 1*, ed. D. A. Martin, SCM Press 1968

Turner, B., 'Institutional Persistence and Ecumenicalism in Northern Methodism', *A Sociological Yearbook of Religion in Britain 2*, ed. D. A. Martin, SCM Press 1969

Wainwright, D., 'Church and People in new housing areas', *Church Quarterly Review*, January-March 1962, pp. 72–83

Wash on Dearne Survey, 'Church Society and Social Change', Mechanics Institute, Wash on Dearne during 1963–64

Wright, D., 'Attitudes towards the church in Wellingborough', *New Society*, 24 June 1965

[1] Available from Wesley College, Bristol

5. *Priesthood and the Ministry*

Carlton, E., 'The Call: The Concept of Vocation in the Free Church Ministry', *A Sociological Yearbook of Religion in Britain 1*, ed. D. A. Martin, SCM Press 1968

Daniel, M., 'Catholic, evangelical and liberal in the Anglican priesthood', *A Sociological Yearbook of Religion in Britain 1*, ed. D. A. Martin, SCM Press 1968

Daniel, M., 'The Association between churchmanship and the Anglican clergyman's self image', *International Conference of Religious Sociology*, 1967

Drewett, Rev. A. J., 'The Social Status of the ordained minister in the 19th and 20th centuries', *Modern Churchman* Vol. IX, No. 2, January 1966

Morgan, D. H. J., The Social and Educational Background of Anglican Bishops, *British Journal of Sociology*, No. 3, September, 1969

Pickering, W. S. F., 'Problems of role analysis and social change, with special reference to the parish clergy', *International Conference of Religious Sociology*, 1967

Pickering, W. S. F., 'Religion – a leisure-time pursuit', *A Sociological Yearbook of Religion in Britain 1*, ed. D. A. Martin, SCM Press 1968

Pickering, W. S. F., 'A Search for New Sociological Approaches to the Sociological Study of the Priesthood', Unpublished article (University of Newcastle)

Portwood D., Secularization and Sanctification', M. A. Thesis, Keele University 1969

Reckitt, M. B. (ed.), *For Christ and People: studies of 4 socialist priests and Prophets in the Church of England*, SPCK 1968

Rudge, P., *Ministry and Management*, Tavistock Publications 1969

Towler, R., 'The Changing Role of the Clergy', *Downside Symposium*, April 1969

Towler, R., 'Puritan and Anti Puritan: types of vocation to the ordained Ministry', *A Sociological Yearbook of Religion in Britain 2*, ed. D. A. Martin, SCM Press 1969

Towler, R., 'The Changing Status of the Ministry', *Crucible*, May 1968

Wilson, B. R., 'The Pentecostalist Minister: role conflict and status contradictions', *American Journal of Sociology*, 64 (5), March 1959

Zahn, G. C., *Chaplains in the RAF*, Manchester University Press 1969

6. *Religion and Education*

Ainsworth, R., *A study of some aspects of the growth of religious understanding of children between the ages of 5 and 11*, Unpublished dip. ed. dissertation, University of Manchester 1961

Alves, C., *Religion and the Secondary School*, SCM Press 1968

Bowley, A. H. & Townroe, M., *The Spiritual Development of the Child*, Livingstone Press

Brothers, J. B., 'Religious Attitudes of Educated Young Catholics in the Same School', Lumen Vitae, Vol. 19 (2) 1964, pp. 339–48

Corbett, Ann, 'Catholics at School', *New Society*, 28 November 1968

Cruickshank, Marjorie, *Church and State in English Education 1870 to present day*, Macmillan 1963

Daines, J. W., *An enquiry into the methods and effects of religious education in the sixth form*, unpublished Ph.D., University of Nottingham, Inst. of Education 1962

Dawes, R. S., *The concept of God among secondary schools*, unpublished M.A. Thesis, London 1954

Dennis, H. M., *Denominational schools as a political problem in England and Wales 1940–59*, unpublished thesis, University of Oxford

Garrity, F. D., 'A study of some secondary modern school pupils' attitude to religious education', *Religious Education* (56), 1961, pp. 141–43

Gibbs, J. M., 'Anglican–Methodist Relations in the field of Education', *Anglican Methodist Relations*, ed. W. S. F. Pickering, Darton, Longman & Todd 1961

Glassey, W., 'The attitudes of grammar school pupils and their parents to education, religion and sport', *British Journal of Educational Psychology* 15, 1945

Goldman, R., 'Children's spiritual development', *Studies in Education: first years at school*, University of London Inst. of Ed, Evans Bros 1963

Goldman, R., *Religious thinking from childhood to adolescence*, Routledge & Kegan Paul 1964

Goldman, R., 'The Application of Piaget's schema of operational thinking to religious story data by means of the Guttman scalogram', *British Journal of Educational Psychology*, 35 (2) 1965, 158–70

Goldman, R., 'Do we want our children to be taught about God?', *New Society*, 27 May 1965

Harrison, J. F. C., *Learning and Living 1790–1960* Routledge & Kegan Paul 1969

Hebron, M. E., 'The Research into the teaching of religious knowledge', *Studies in Education*, University of Hull 1957

Hilliard, F. H., 'Ideas of God among secondary school children', *Religion in education*, Vol. 27, No. 1

Hilliard, F. H., 'The Influences of religious education upon the development of children's moral ideas', *British Journal of Educational Psychology*, 29, pp. 50–59

Johnson, J. E., *An enquiry into some of the religious ideas of 6-year-old children*, unpublished Dip. Ed. thesis, University of Birmingham

May, P. R. & Johnston, O. R., 'Parental Attitudes to Religious Education in State Schools', *Durham Research Review*, No. 18, April 1967

Moreton, F. E., *A brief consideration of religious experience*, unpublished Ph.D., Birmingham 1931

Moreton, F. E., 'Attitudes to religion amongst adolescents and adults', *British Journal of Educational Psychology*, 1944

Oliva, R. A. & Butcher, H. J., 'Teacher's attitude to Education', *Journal of Educational Psychology*, 38 (1), 1968

Oxtoby, M. and Smith, B., 'Students entering Sussex and Essex Universities in 1966: some similarities and differences', *Research in Education*, May 1969

Rees, R. J., *Background and Belief*, SCM Press 1967

Rison, L. D., *An experiment and critical study of the teaching of scripture in secondary schools*, unpublished Ph.D., University of London 1959
Spencer, A. E. C. W., 'An evaluation of Roman Catholic Education Policy in England and Wales, 1900–1960', *Religious Education*, ed. P. Jebb, Darton, Longman–Todd 1968
Vincent, P., 'Glasgow Jewish school children', *Jewish Journal of Sociology*, Vol. 6 (2). December 1964
Vincent, P., 'The measured intelligence of Glasgow Jewish school children', *Jewish Journal of Sociology*, Vol. 8 (1), June 1966
Walker, D. J. C., *A Study of children's conception of God*, unpublished Ed. D. Thesis, University of Glasgow 1950
Wright, D. S., 'A Study of religious belief in sixth form boys', *Research and Studies*, No. 24, Institute of Education, University of Leeds, October 1962
Wright, D. & Cox, E., 'A Study of the relationship between moral judgement and religious belief in a sample of English Adolescents', *Journal of Social Psychology*, 72 (1) 1967

7. *Religion and Politics*

Alexander, K. J. W. & Hobbs, A., 'What Influences Labour MPs?' *Studies in British Politics*, ed. R. Rose, Macmillan 1966
Alford, R. R., *Party and Society*, Rand & McNally, Chicago 1963
Barritt, D. P. & Carter, C. F., *The Northern Ireland Problem*, OUP 1962
Benney, H. Gray & Pear, *How People Vote: A Study of Behaviour in Greenwich*, Routledge & Kegan Paul 1956
Boserup, Anders & Weisen, Claus, *Rank Analysis of a Polarized Community – a case study of Northern Ireland*, Inst. of Peace and Conflict Research, Copenhagen 1967 – Vol. 8 of papers of Peace Research Society
Bromhead, P. A., *The House of Lords and Contemporary Politics 1911–57*, Routledge & Kegan Paul 1958, pp. 53–67
Butler, D. E. & Stokes, D., *Political Change in Britain*, Macmillan 1969
Campbell, C. B., Davidson & Potter, *Voting Behaviour in Droylesden in October 1951*, Manchester School, 1952
Every, G., 'The present form of establishment', *Church Quarterly Review*, April 1962
Harman, L., 'Sociology of the Establishment', *Prism* 1966
Henson, H. H., 'Ought establishment to be maintained?' *Political quarterly*, September 1930
Heubel, E. J., 'Church and State in England, the price of the establishment', *Western Political Quarterly*, vol. 18 (3), September 1965
Hinchcliffe, P., *The One-sided reciprocity – a study in the modification of the establishment*, Darton, Longman & Todd 1966
Hill, M., 'The English Voter – 1', *New Society*, 17 September 1964
Hill, M., 'Official Attitudes of the British Churches to the War in Vietnam', unpublished paper, LSE 1968

Howes, G., *The Established Church and social change in East Anglia, 1750–1850*, Research in Progress, University of Cambridge

Jenkins, R. & MacRae, J., Religious conflict and polarization in Northern Ireland Peace research centre, Lancaster 1966

Jenkins, R., 'Religion and Conflict in Northern Ireland', *A Sociological Yearbook of Religion in Britain 2*, ed. D. A. Martin, SCM Press 1969

Milne, R. S. & MacKenzie, W. C., *Marginal Seat: voting in Bristol N. E.*, Hansard Society 1958

Nordlinger, E. A., *Working Class Tories*, MacGibbon & Kee 1967

Pear, R. F., 'The Liberal Vote', *Pol. Quarterly*, July–September 1962

Potter, A., *Organised groups in British National Politics*, Faber & Faber 1961

Richard, P. G., *Patronage in British Government*, Allen & Unwin 1963

Rose, R., *Politics in England*, Faber & Faber 1965, esp. ch. 3

Rowse, A. L., 'The dilemma of Church and State', *Political Quarterly*, July 1936

Welsh, P. J., 'Bloomfield and Peel: a study in co-operation between Church and State, 1841–46', *Journal of Ecclesiastical History*, Vol. 12 1961, pp. 71 ff.

8. *Sects and Specialized Groups*

Benedict, B., *Two Religious Associations in London – Muslim (Woking) and Buddhist*, unpublished Ph.D., London 1954

Budd, S., 'The Humanist Societies: the Consequences of a Diffuse Belief System', *Patterns of Sectarianism*, (ed.) B. R. Wilson, Heineman, 1967

Butterworth, E., *A Muslim Community in Britain*, Church Information Office, London 1967

Calley, M. J. C., *God's People*, OUP 1965

Campbell, C. B., *Humanism and the Culture of the Professions: A Study of the rise of the British Humanist Movement 1954–63*, unpublished Ph.D. Thesis, London 1967

Campbell, C. B., 'Humanism in Britain: the formation of a secular value oriented movement', *A Sociological Yearbook of Religion in Britain 1*, ed. D. A. Martin, SCM Press 1968

Child, J., 'Quaker Employers and Industrial Relations', *Sociological Review*, Vol. 12 (3), November 1964

Connell, J. H., *The Distribution and Migration of the Jewish Population of Leeds*, unpublished B.A. Dissertation, University of London

Embley, P. L., 'The Early Development of the Plymouth Brethren', *Patterns of Sectarianism*, ed. B. R. Wilson, Heinemann 1967

Eros, J., 'The Rise of Organised Freethought in Mid-Victorian England', *Sociological Review*, 2 (1), 1954

Friedman, M. (ed.), *A Minority in Britain*, Vallentine, Mitchell & Co. 1955

Friedman, M., 'The Jewish Population of Great Britain', *Jewish Journal of Sociology*, June 1962

Gartner, L. P., 'From Jewish Immigrant to English Jew', *New Society*, 2 September 1965

Gould, J. & Esh, S. (eds.), *Jewish Life in Modern Britain*, Routledge & Kegan Paul 1964

Ishichei, E. A., 'Organisation and power in the Society of Friends 1852–59', *Patterns of Sectarianism*, ed. B. R. Wilson, Heinemann 1967

Jackson, J. & Jobling, R., 'Towards the analysis of Contemporary Cults', *A Sociological Yearbook of Religion in Britain 1*, ed. D. A. Martin, SCM Press 1968

De Kadt, E. J., 'On locating minority group members: two British surveys of Jewish university students', *Jewish Journal of Sociology*, Vol. 6 (i), 1964

Kiev, A., 'Psychotherapeutic aspects of Pentecostalist sects amongst West Indian to England', *British Journal of Sociology*, 15 (2), 1964

Krausz, E., 'An Anglo-Jewish community: Leeds', *Jewish Journal of Sociology*, Vol. 3 (i), 1961

Krausz, E., 'Occupation and advancement in Anglo-jewry', *Jewish Journal of Sociology*, Vol. 4 (1), 1962

Krausz, E., *Leeds Jewry: its history and social structure*, Heffer & Sons 1964

MacInnes, C., 'Five Faiths', *New Society*, 6 April 1967

Mackworth, C., 'Les Catholiques Anglais', Preuves, fevrier-mars 1969

Martin, B., 'The Spiritualist Meeting' (unpublished)

Needham, B., *Unitarian Congregations surveyed*, London Gen. Ass. of Unitarian and Free Churches, 1967

Nelson, G. K., 'The analysis of a cult: Spiritualism', *Social Compass* 15 (6), Nov. 1968

Nelson, G. K., *Spiritualism*, Routledge & Kegan Paul 1968

Nelson, G. K., 'The Concept of a Cult', *Sociological Review*, 1968

Robertson, R., 'The Salvation army: the persistence of sectarianism', *Patterns of Sectarianism*, ed. B. R. Wilson, Heinemann 1967

Warburton, T. R., *A Comparative Study of Minority Religious Groups: with special reference to Holiness and related movements in Britain in the last Fifty Years*, unpublished Ph.D., London, 1966

Warburton, T. R., 'Organisation and change in a British Holiness Movement', *Patterns of Sectarianism*, ed. B. R. Wilson, Heinemann 1967

Warburton, T. R., 'Holiness Religion: An anomaly of Sectarian Typologies', *Journal for the Scientific Study of Religion* VIII (1), 1969

Willis, Gordon & Wilson, B. R., 'The Churches of God: Pattern and Practice', *Patterns of Sectarianism*, ed. B. R. Wilson, Heinemann 1967

Wilson, B. R., 'The Exclusive Brethren: A case study in the evolution of a sectarian ideology', *Patterns of Sectarianism*, ed. B. R. Wilson, Heinemann 1967

Wilson, J., 'British Israelism: the ideological restraints on sect organization', *Patterns of Sectarianism*, ed. B. R. Wilson, Heinemann 1967

Wilson, J., 'British Israelism', *Sociological Review*, 16 (1) 1969 pp. 41–59

9. *Research in Progress*

Absalom, J., *Anglo-Catholicism: Ideology and Influence*, Research in Progress, M.Phil., London

Bridges, Rev. P., *Religious Census of Hemel Hempstead*, Research in Progress, University of Birmingham, Department of Architecture

Carter, D., *Social and Political Influences of Bristol Churches, 1828–1914*, Research in Progress, University of Bristol

Coles, R. W., *Patterns of Culture and Commitment in the Church of England*, Research in Progress, D.Phil., University of York

Coles, R. W., *A Social Analysis of Religion in Britain*, Research in Progress for the Archbishops' Commission on Church and State

Foster, B., *A Study of Patterns of Christian Commitment*, Research in Progress, University of Birmingham

Gaine, M. B., *Anti-semitism as a function of religious education*, Research in Progress, Christ College, Liverpool

Gay, J., *The Social Geography of Religion in Britain*, Research in Progress, D. Phil., Oxford. To be published. Has extensive bibliography

Goodridge, R. M., *Comparative religious practice of 19th Century Bristol and Marseille*, M.Phil. thesis, London 1969

Hill, M., *The History and Structure of Anglican Religious Orders*, Research in Progress, D.Phil., Oxford

Hillyer, Ruth, *The Parson's Wife*, M.Phil. thesis in Progress at King's College, London

Hinings, C. R., *The Clun Valley Survey*, Research in Progress, University of Birmingham

McCleod, D. H., *Membership and Influence of the Churches in Metropolitan London 1885–1914*, Research in Progress, Ph.D., Cambridge

Moore, R. S., *Social and Political roles of Methodism in the Deerness Valley (1870–1970)*, Research in Progress, University of Durham

Patterson, Sheila, *A Study of Migration to England*, Research in Progress, Institute of Race Relations

Paul, L., *The St George's House Survey: the role and attitudes of the clergy*, Research in Progress, Queens College, Birmingham

Pickering, W. S. F., *A sociological study of the place of married students (and their wives) in theological colleges in Britain*, Research in Progress, Dept. of Social Studies, University of Newcastle

Rees, D. Ben, *Social and Industrial Reasons for the Decline of Welsh Nonconformity, with Special Reference to the Aberdare Valley in Glamorganshire*, M.Sc. in progress (address: 32 Garth Road, Liverpool 18.)

Robinson, T., *The Formation of the Church of England Board of Social responsibility*, Research in Progress, University of Sheffield

Scharf, Betty R., *Analysis of theories of sectarian Christianity, with special reference to the Roman Catholic Church*, Research in Progress, LSE

Scribbins, K., *Aspects of Secularization in the second half of the 19th century in Britain*, M.Phil. research in progress at LSE